Praise for *Becky N*

"*Becky Nurse of Salem* seeks to move shadows to the ~~light~~, a mischievous, sprightly alternative narrative to the patriarchal one handed down by American history books, by Arthur Miller's *The Crucible*, by the way men still talk about and treat women . . . For that invigorating feeling, we can thank the one-of-a-kind voice and vision of Ruhl, who writes with sweeping imagination and puckish glee, yet at a twinkly remove."

—LILY JANIAK, *SAN FRANCISCO CHRONICLE*

"Ruhl's smart script links the witch hunts of Salem to the #MeToo, 'Lock her up' misogyny of Trumpist rhetoric in the 2016 election in a wickedly dark comedy with sinister socio-political and economic implications . . . Not much has changed since the seventeenth century and Ruhl drives home this point in a rich, complex work."

—STEVE MURRAY, *BROADWAY WORLD*

"The heart of the play is this running theme of women's pain and generational trauma . . . It's very moving."

—NPR, *ARTSCAPE*

"If it's been a while since you read *The Crucible*, you'll get a fabulous refresher from playwright Sarah Ruhl in *Becky Nurse of Salem* . . . Becky Nurse isn't built on Miller's drama, though setting the play in Salem does give Ruhl the chance to cleverly respond to the sixty-nine-year-old piece . . . More than three centuries later, women are still trying to prove they aren't witches!"

—MELISSA ROSE BERNARDO, *NEW YORK STAGE REVIEW*

"Ruhl takes *The Crucible* to task alongside the way society, including other women, denounces those who dare to feel to the extreme and do something about it . . . Neither historical nor current witch hunts were ever about the supernatural, but about the very natural experience of being a woman with power."

—GILLIAN RUSSO, *NEW YORK THEATRE GUIDE*

"There's much to say about *Becky Nurse of Salem*, for Sarah Ruhl has embedded layer upon layer of meaning and connection and social commentary into a story that never flags and never betrays the audience's attention . . . A magnificent work of theatrical art."

—PATRICK THOMAS, *TALKIN' BROADWAY*

"Ruhl is unearthing the past to examine, and make sense of what went wrong . . . She wakes Miller's play up by reshaping it with a damaged, yet sympathetic woman as the protagonist."

—IDA MOJADAD, *SF WEEKLY*

"Sarah Ruhl rules! The MacArthur Fellowship 'genius' award winner's latest play is a thoroughly captivating, charming and ultimately satisfying quirky comedy that ponders the Salem witch trials and much more. With humor and insight, *Becky Nurse of Salem* explores family dynamics, contemporary politics, feminism, opiate addiction and how Arthur Miller's infatuation with Marilyn Monroe influenced his 1953 landmark opus, *The Crucible*."

—EMILY S. MENDEL, *BERKELEYSIDE*

"A complex and darkly funny look at the Salem witch trials through the lens of contemporary American malaise, the #MeToo movement, and Donald Trump . . . Ruhl wants to make sure, above all, that audiences walk away remembering that women were at the heart of the mass hysteria of 1692. A fine and funny work from a playwright still at the top of her game."

—JAY BARMANN, *SFIST*

"A crackling new play . . . *Becky Nurse of Salem* didn't happen in a vacuum. It happened because Sarah felt she had to write something about the times we live in . . . This is Sarah Ruhl at her finest, and most astute, and *Becky Nurse of Salem* is a brilliant play—thought-provoking, very funny, with something to chew on in nearly every single scene."

—RICHARD WOLINSKY, *KPFA*

BECKY NURSE OF SALEM

◆

BECKY NURSE OF SALEM

◆

A CONTEMPORARY COMEDY
ABOUT A HISTORICAL TRAGEDY

SARAH RUHL

THEATRE COMMUNICATIONS GROUP
NEW YORK
2024

Credits: (Page 7) "The Lovers," *Don't Go Back to Sleep* by Timothy Liu. Copyright © 2014 (Ardmore, PA: Saturnalia Books). Used by permission of Timothy Liu. (Pages 7, 149–150) *The Crucible* by Arthur Miller. Copyright © 1952, 1953, 1954, renewed © 1980, 1981, 1982 by Arthur Miller. Used by permission of Viking Books, an imprint of Penguin Publishing Group, a division of Penguin Random House LLC. All rights reserved. (Page 149) "Why I Wrote *The Crucible*" by Arthur Miller. Copyright © 1996 by Arthur Miller, used by permission of The Wylie Agency LLC.

The publication of *Becky Nurse of Salem* by Sarah Ruhl, through TCG Books, is made possible with support by Mellon Foundation.

Special thanks to Julie Morris for her generous support of this publication.

TCG books are exclusively distributed to the book trade by Consortium Book Sales and Distribution.

Library of Congress Control Numbers:
2023019616 (print) / 2023019617 (ebook)
ISBN 978-1-55936-987-9 (paperback) / ISBN 978-1-55936-946-6 (ebook)
A catalog record for this book is available from the Library of Congress.

Book design and composition by Lisa Govan
Cover design by John Gall
Cover art: J.E. Baker.Library of Congress

First Edition, March 2024

For all the so-called witches who got hanged with no proper burial,
for all the women who are still called witches in our place and our time,
for all the young girls who played Abigail in the school play,
and for my grandmother, Kay Kehoe.

◆

BECKY NURSE OF SALEM

◆

PRODUCTION HISTORY

A staged reading of *Becky Nurse of Salem* was developed and presented by New York Stage and Film (Chris Burney, Artistic Director) at Vassar College's Martel Theater in Poughkeepsie, New York, on July 19, 2019. It was directed by Sarah Ruhl. The cast was:

BECKY	Ann McDonough
BOB	Brian Kerwin
GAIL	Susannah Perkins
A WITCH	Polly Noonan
STAN	David McElwee
SHELBY	Miriam Silverman
SHAPE SHIFTER	Mark Bedard

Becky Nurse of Salem had its world premiere at Berkeley Repertory Theatre (Johanna Pfaelzer, Artistic Director; Susan Medak, Managing Director) in Berkeley, California, on December 19, 2019. It was directed by Anne Kauffman. The set design was by Louisa Thompson, the costume design was by Meg Neville, the lighting design was by Russell H. Champa, the sound design was by Mikaal Sulaiman, the original music was by Daniel Kluger; the dramaturg was Madeleine Oldham and the production stage manager was Michael Suenkel. The cast was:

BECKY	Pamela Reed
BOB	Adrian Roberts

GAIL	Naian González Norvind
A WITCH	Ruibo Qian
STAN	Owen Campbell
SHELBY	Elissa Beth Stebbins
SHAPE SHIFTER	Rod Gnapp

Becky Nurse of Salem had its New York premiere at Lincoln Center Theater (André Bishop, Producing Artistic Director; Adam Siegel, Managing Director) on December 4, 2022. It was directed by Rebecca Taichman. The set design was by Riccardo Hernández, the costume design was by Emily Rebholz, the lighting design was by Barbara Samuels, the sound design was by Palmer Hefferan, the original music was by Suzzy Roche, the projection design was by Tal Yarden; the production stage manager was Caroline Englander. The cast was:

BECKY	Deirdre O'Connell
BOB	Bernard White
GAIL	Alicia Crowder
A WITCH	Candy Buckley
STAN	Julian Sanchez
SHELBY	Tina Benko
THE JAILER / THE JUDGE	Thomas Jay Ryan

CHARACTERS

1. BECKY. Our hero, descended from Rebecca Nurse on one side. In her mid-fifties to sixties.
2. BOB. The man she loves. In his mid-fifties to sixties.
3. GAIL. Becky's granddaughter. Also plays Abigail in Act Two. In her teens but can be played by an actress in her twenties.
4. A WITCH. A woman in her sixties to eighties.
5. STAN. A little bit androgynous. Seventeen or eighteen but can be played by an actor in his twenties.
6. SHELBY. Has several degrees in art history. Thirties.
7. THE JAILER / THE JUDGE. Virtuosic performer; plays jailer, magistrate, creepy voices, and judge. A man in his thirties to fifties.

PLACE

Salem, Massachusetts.

SET

Many places can be indicated with one or two objects and light, without sketching in the details. For example, a bar is just a cash register on a counter. Scenes move fluidly. Subtitles might be used in scene titles to indicate location.

Act One

A museum with wax figures and weird historical dioramas.
Bob's bar counter.
A Marriott hotel counter.
Becky's living room, which might be just an old couch and a sweet
old broken lamp.
A psychic's table.
A hospital room.
The town square.

Act Two

The town square.
The town jail: an empty cell with a bench, a desk and a chair for the
jailer, and an open area for visitors.
A courtroom.
And the outdoors, near a parking lot and an open sky.

TIME

Act One: 2016 and an imagined 1692.
Act Two: 2017 and an imagined 1692.

You are pulling Heaven down and raising up a whore!

—ARTHUR MILLER, *THE CRUCIBLE*

I was always afraid / of the next card / the psychic would turn / over for us—Forgive me / for not knowing / how we were / every card in the deck.

—TIMOTHY LIU, "THE LOVERS"

ACT ONE

Scene 1 — At the Museum. A Tour.

Becky at the museum where she leads a group of schoolchildren.

BECKY

My name is Becky Nurse and I'll be your tour guide.

In the dark, a not-very-subtle voice comes on, possibly with creepy music underneath:

CREEPY VOICE

Do you believe in witches? Your ancestors did . . . Welcome to the Salem Museum of Witchcraft.

BECKY

Okay. I'm actually related to Rebecca Nurse—one of the so-called witches—you can see her in this wax statue.

Lights up on a weird wax statue of an old woman in Pilgrim attire.

I'm like her great-great-great-great-great-something once removed. Lucille Ball's related to her too. Fact. Mitt Romney too. Fact. Fun family reunions. Just kidding, I was never invited. Anyway, Rebecca Nurse was this old pious woman, a little hard of hearing in one ear. You might say she was put to death because she couldn't hear the judge's question.

She gestures to an invisible diorama with wax figures.

And here you'll see a wax figure of John Proctor. You must know of him from that play *The Crucible*. *(Pause, a child says they haven't read* The Crucible*)* No—you haven't read *The Crucible?* I thought every high school kid had to read it. No?

Okay. Well, then I'll tell you the story of it. It's like our goddamn Christmas pageant here in Salem.

It goes like this:

Little Betty is lying in kind of a coma. But she keeps heading to the window to fly out. Her father is concerned. So they call a doctor. Meanwhile, Abigail, the niece, who is described as a "beautiful dissembler" in the play (basically, she's an actress), comes in. So Abigail admits that she and her friends have been dancing naked in the forest. Abigail's worried she'll get in trouble for dancing naked in the forest. So she wakes up Betty. And Betty says Abigail drank blood to kill John Proctor's pregnant wife. Abigail says, Shut it, Betty. We just danced naked in the forest and tried to talk to dead babies and *that's it.*

Now, in the *play*, the reason Abigail wanted to get revenge on John Proctor's pregnant wife (this is what I could never really wrap my head around) is that this young girl wants to fuck an old man— sorry, sleep with?

You guys are in high school, you know all about this stuff. Anyway, in the play Abigail was seventeen but in real life she was eleven. Fact. In the play he's like: "You whore! Stop tempting me." And I'm

like, um, she's eleven. More likely that John Proctor molested—
(Sees a teacher who looks disapproving) Sorry—courted—Abigail.

Let's move on.

She gestures to another invisible diorama.

Now Tituba was the first woman to confess to witchcraft, which
was the practical thing to do, because if you didn't confess, you got
hung. It's like, some white Pilgrim lady asked Tituba to do a spell
and then called her a witch for doing it. Sort of like an old man
asking a little girl to perform a sex act and then calling her a whore.

Now, here you'll see the courtroom where these bewitched girls
started having these weird fits.

Thrashing around—it was *violent*. Like one even dislocated an
elbow. And the girls start naming the women in the town as witches,
like Sarah Good, a single mother without a lot of money. She was
said to mutter after begging. Like she'd knock on your door and
say, "Can I have a potato? Or some firewood?" And people would
say no. And she'd go off muttering, "You goddamn selfish piece
of shit." And people thought she was cursing them. Her daughter
Dorcas who was five had to come to jail with her, and poor little
Dorcas went crazy in jail. I mean who puts a child in a cage with
her mother?

*This is a disturbing thought. Becky recovers. Someone asks her a question
that we don't hear: Don't some people say that the girls were poisoned
by rye bread?*

What's that? Yeah, some people say the girls' jerking around looks
like rye bread poisoning.

I'd like to write my own play of the Salem witch trials. I'd have a
woman baking bread for half an hour. Then I'd show three girls
eating it. Then I'd show them acting really strange. Then I'd show
a lot of women getting hung from a tree.

I'll take you to the gift shop now.

Scene 2 — Bob's Tavern. Lock Her Up.

Becky at a local bar.
A bartender named Bob pours a beer for her.
A TV is on, with a Trump rally blaring.

CROWD
(From the TV) Lock her up! Lock her up! Lock her up!

BECKY
Can you turn that shit off, Bob?

Bob turns it off.

Ugh, the world is so loud—

BOB
You okay, Becky?
You tired?

BECKY

Tired of giving tours, maybe.

BOB

What else would you do?

BECKY

Move.

BOB

Leave Salem?

BECKY

Sure, leave Salem.

BOB

I've known you too long, Becky. You're not leaving Salem.

BECKY

I could!

BOB

So where would you go?

BECKY

I don't know—Idaho?

BOB

Who would you know in goddamn Idaho?

BECKY

No one. That's the point. No one would know me as the descendent of Rebecca Nurse, slightly deaf witch hung on Gallows Hill, which is now the site of a Dunkin' Donuts.

BOB

Gallows Hill was not at the Dunkin' Donuts.

BECKY

Bob, it is. Not the Dunkin' Donuts on Main Street—the other Dunkin' Donuts.

13

BOB

Bad coffee with a shitload of sugar.

BECKY

You a snob now?

BOB

No . . .

BECKY

I'm not a coffee drinker. Too bitter.

BOB

Sure you don't like bitter things?

BECKY

Yeah, I hate myself cuz I'm too bitter. Ha ha.

BOB

Well, I heard they invented coffee so Sufi poets could stay awake all night having mystical experiences and writing poetry and now we just drink it to get through the day.

BECKY

Where the hell did you hear that, Bob?

BOB

PBS. PBS has great documentaries.

BECKY

The point is: the postcards I sell at the museum—that scary looking tree, with evil arms pointing to the sky? It's not where they hung the witches, it's just some tree. Gallows Hill is at the exact site of the old Dunkin' Donuts.

BOB

Nope, not my Dunkin's.

BECKY

THE OTHER DUNKIN' DONUTS, Bob.

BOB

If you say so. I heard it was at the Walgreens.

BECKY

Who the hell have you been talking to, Bob? I hate that goddamn Walgreens. Anyway, my new boss annoys the shit out of me.

BOB

I love office politics. You own your own business, you got no villains. Sometimes you need a villain to get through your day.

BECKY

So you say. But you don't have to deal with *Shelby*.

BOB

What's wrong with Shelby?

BECKY

Oh, she's so . . . *(Makes a face)* smug. And she's cutting jobs and putting in more videos so you don't need real people to give tours anymore. You just press the button and some creepy voice says: "Do you believe in witches? Your ancestors did." They hired her when Donna got the cancer and the board wants the museum to make money. Who ever heard of a frigging museum that turned a profit? And she wants me to follow the script all the time.

BOB

You don't follow the script?

BECKY

Well, the script bores me sometimes and then I deviate slightly.

BOB

Oh—well I could see where that would be—maybe a mild irritation for her. If your job is to follow the script.

BECKY

I know more than Shelby about the witch trials. That's the trouble. I know too much. She might be a professor, but if she were a good

15

professor she'd be teaching at a college, right—not working at the Salem Museum of freaking Witchcraft. And she wears—these—*blouses*—with these little *ties*—she thinks she's better than everyone in town—she thinks Gallows Hill was down by the Walgreens because someone at frigging Harvard said so, but if you're from this town you know that Gallows Hill is at the goddamn Dunkin' Donuts! In the exact spot where you eat your morning jelly roll—

BOB

I hate jelly rolls—it's disconcerting when jelly flies into your mouth—

BECKY

Right, fine, or your CRUELLER— Some poor woman was being hanged. And denied a burial. With her daughters watching and weeping their eyes out.

Pause.
Becky is sad.

BOB

How is Gail doing?

BECKY

Oh, a little better.

BOB

When's she coming home from the hospital?

BECKY

They won't say. Once you get in there, it's up to the shrinks when you get out.

BOB

Right.

BECKY

Sometimes I worry so goddamn much it takes up my whole goddamn life. I don't know if I was cut out to be a mother. Or a grandmother. Or whatever the hell I am.

BOB

You were definitely cut out to be a mother.

BECKY

Thanks, Bob. I didn't exactly succeed at it. If you judge by outcome.

BOB

I don't judge by outcome.

BECKY

Then how would you know?

BOB

I can tell. From your worry.

BECKY

Oh right, from my white hairs?

BOB

You don't have any white hairs.

Becky shows him a white hair.

BECKY

See?

BOB

Your hair smells good—like orange juice.

BECKY

Thanks. I dip it in my goddamn Tropicana every morning.

BOB

You do?

BECKY

No. I better get back to work. Lunch break's over.

BOB

This one's on me.

Scene 3 — At the Museum.

SHELBY

The schoolteachers were very troubled when you said "fuck."

BECKY

I'm sorry, it just slipped out. I corrected myself and said "sleep with." Immediately.

SHELBY

And "whore"?

BECKY

The word "whore" is in *The Crucible* like eight times, for Chrissake, and it's required reading.

SHELBY

In any case, today's group was from a Catholic school. The nuns complained.

BECKY

Oh— Well . . . nuns . . . you know.

SHELBY

Do you have your lunch at the bar?

BECKY

Sometimes.

SHELBY

Do you drink by any chance on your lunch break?

BECKY

Drink what?

SHELBY

Alcohol.

BECKY

I have a ploughman's lunch. Pickles and cheese. It comes with beer on the side.

SHELBY

Well, regardless, we just can't have you going off script. We have thousands of schoolchildren here every week. We're going to have to let you go, Becky.

BECKY

Let me go? I've worked here for twenty years, and my God, I'm *from here*. I know more about the trials than anyone in this town. I may not have a college degree, but I should be running this museum by now.

Shelby smiles.

Are you laughing at me?

SHELBY

No, it's just—you'd need a college degree to run a museum, I'd imagine.

BECKY

You are such a bitch.

SHELBY

You're fired.

BECKY

You can't fire me.

SHELBY

You just called me a bitch, Becky. What do you expect?

BECKY

I shouldn't have said that.

SHELBY

You can clear out your desk by the end of the day.

BECKY

I don't have a fucking desk.

SHELBY

Well that makes it easier, I guess.

BECKY

My own ancestor was hung in this town!

SHELBY

Hanged.

BECKY

What?

SHELBY

People are hanged, paintings are hung.

BECKY

Jesus Christ, I have to support my granddaughter.

SHELBY

That's beyond my purview.

BECKY

Your purview is to fill up the goddamn gift shop with Harry Potter trinkets and fire the locals to save money. Because no one wants to remember a goddamn atrocity in this country until they can make a buck from it. You know what's wrong with people like you?

SHELBY

People like me?

BECKY

Yeah, people like you. You act like you care about other women on paper but when it comes to actual women you toss them under the bus.

SHELBY

Becky, I don't believe in people like you and people like me. We need to lift each other up. That's what this museum should be about, teaching women not to accuse each other, and not to be divided by the patriarchy.

BECKY

What about my health insurance?

SHELBY

I believe you can purchase COBRA for six months.

BECKY

I'm taking Rebecca Nurse with me.

SHELBY

You can't take the wax works—

BECKY

She's my birthright—

21

SHELBY

Becky!

BECKY

She belongs with me and my family—

SHELBY

Security!

Becky runs out with the wax statue.

Scene 4—The Pilgrims and the Homebodies.

Bob pours Becky a drink at the bar.

BECKY

I can't afford fucking COBRA. And with my own health crap, and
Gail in and out of the hospital—

BOB

Did you ask politely for your job back?

BECKY

I called her a bitch and ran out with a wax statue.

BOB

You're lucky she didn't press charges.

BECKY

She called a security guard, so I gave it back.

BOB

You're always going and shooting yourself in the foot. Why do you do that?

BECKY

I get so mad. Sometimes I walk around thinking: I'd like to take my shoe off and just throw it at a person.

A moment.

You got the classifieds here?

BOB

Yup.

BECKY

Thanks.
Let's see . . .
Full-time nurse, nope—
Overnight clerk at the Marriott . . . I could do that . . .

BOB

I need my sleep, personally.

BECKY

I like my sleep, but I need the money, personally.
Bob—does it ever make you mad how hard it is to live and get by?

BOB

I'm not really an angry person.

BECKY

No, you're not. Remember, in high school, when you and the guys let a greased pig out in the cafeteria as a prank and you got all the blame for it? Because you were left holding the Crisco? You never squealed on them, and you didn't get mad, even though you got expelled before graduation.

BOB

Yup.

BECKY

Ever wonder how your life woulda turned out different if it weren't for that?

BOB

Uh, yeah. I'd never have run my in-laws' bar, for one thing. I always wanted to be a history teacher. I always wanted to move somewhere—sunny. California, maybe. That's funny, right? I wanted to be a history teacher in a place with a little less history.

BECKY

I think you could divide up the world into two types of people—those who leave the town of their birth, and those who don't.

BOB

What about those who leave and come back?

BECKY

True. There are those who are buried in the same ground where they were born, and those that are buried way far away. The pilgrims, and the homebodies. Why the fuck didn't I leave Salem when I had the chance?

BOB

Gail will be a grown-up before you know it. Then you could fly away.

BECKY

At the end of the day, I think I'm one of those who gets buried where she was born. One foot away from my mother. One foot away from my daughter. Hopefully Gail will get the hell out.

A pause. Bob doesn't know what to say.

I'm going to go see about that Marriott job.

Scene 5 — The Night Shift. Marriott Hotel.

BECKY

I'm here about the overnight job.

STAN

Sorry, it's already filled.

BECKY

That fast?

STAN

Yeah, by me. Sorry.

BECKY

Goddammit!

STAN

You wouldn't want this job. It's lonely and I see crazy shit here at night. Shit you wouldn't believe.

BECKY

Like what?

STAN

It's like Halloween all year long in Salem. People get messed up, go play in the graveyard, come here to party all night. They're like, possessed. Between the pills and everything else, they're jerking around, falling over, and last night I'm at the front desk calling 911, and it's like, scary.

BECKY

You did call 911 though?

STAN

Yeah, of course.

BECKY

Good, you should.

STAN

I did.

BECKY

Okay. Well, there're only two jobs in Salem and this is the only one I'm qualified for.

STAN

Sorry.

BECKY

Oh well.

She turns to leave.

STAN

Hey. You know how I got this job?

BECKY

How?

27

STAN

I went to see a witch.

BECKY

Seriously?

STAN

Yeah, within a day of seeing her—boom, I got this job. You want her number?

BECKY

Nah. I don't see witches.

STAN

Why not?

BECKY

My ancestor was killed because of all this witch stuff.

STAN

Seriously? Was she a witch?

BECKY

No.

STAN

Oh. Well, you need a job, see this lady.

BECKY

Is there a money-back guarantee?

STAN

What have you got to lose?

BECKY

Money.

STAN

Well yeah. But here's her card if you want it.

He hands her a card.

Scene 6 — Becky Visits a Witch.

The Psychic Witch's Emporium on Main Street.

BECKY

And then I got fired.

WITCH

So you're looking for a new job?

BECKY

Yeah.

WITCH

Good, I don't do revenge.

BECKY

I didn't say revenge.

WITCH

For the new job part, burn these, then put the ashes under your pillow.

The witch gives her a little package.

BECKY

Okay.

WITCH

I can also see that you lack love in your life.

BECKY

I didn't come here for that.

WITCH

I see that you once had a love, but it was a very painful love. Is this right?

BECKY

Yes.

WITCH

I see that you have some bad luck in your life, caused by a curse, way back.

BECKY

My great-great-great-great-grandmother is Rebecca Nurse.

WITCH

Oh no! That's bad.

BECKY

Yeah.

WITCH

We have to remove that curse.

BECKY

Can you do that?

WITCH

Yes. For four hundred dollars.

BECKY

Jesus, four hundred dollars!

WITCH

To remove a curse like that, as old as that, I have to do rituals non-stop for a week.

BECKY

I don't have that kind of money.

WITCH

I can also see you're worried about a young woman. Your daughter? No. Your daughter is not with us. Am I right or wrong?

BECKY

Right.

WITCH

Then your granddaughter. Am I right?

BECKY

Oh goddammit.

WITCH

You're worried that what happened to your daughter will happen to your granddaughter. Am I right?

Becky nods.

We can't mess around with this.
We have to remove that curse.
I can see you hesitating. Becky—don't worry—I only use my power for good, not for evil. You have to trust me. Do you trust me?

BECKY

Okay.

WITCH

You have to follow all my instructions to the letter. And don't tell anyone what you're doing. When can you get me the four hundred dollars by?

BECKY

Tomorrow, I guess.

WITCH

Okay. In the meantime, what do you have?

Becky pulls out some crumpled bills, all the money in her wallet.

BECKY

I have fourteen dollars.

WITCH

Okay, put it here. So we can start the process.

Becky puts down her cash.

Good. Thank you.
Money is not really money, it just symbolizes your intention.
Hold my hands over the cash.
Now, feel that this money symbolizes your intention to be in love, to be happy, to use your power for good, and to save your grand-daughter.

They hold hands over the cash.

I also see a man.

BECKY

A man?

WITCH

Yes, a man you were destined to love, but your paths diverged, when you were young. Am I right?

BECKY

You mean Bob?

WITCH

Yes, Bob.

BECKY

Nah, Bob's just a friend.

WITCH

Becky. I know, I see.
Put these crystals somewhere near him, but so he can't see them.

She gives Becky a little pouch of crystals.

BECKY

I told you, I didn't come here for love.

WITCH

But they all come for love. Every last one of them.
Come back tomorrow and I'll give you a love ointment.

BECKY

Fine.

WITCH

Now for your granddaughter, make a nice big fire, and burn these in it.

The witch gives Becky a pouch of herbs.

And say some words over the fire.

BECKY

Like a spell?

WITCH

You think the universe can hear what you want if you don't say it out loud?
You did good, Becky. You're going to be all right.

The witch takes Becky's hands. Becky nods.

It's good you came to me when you did. If you hadn't . . . *(The witch shakes her head)*
Bad. Bad. Bad.

Scene 7 — Becky Asks Bob for Money. Bob's Tavern.

BOB

Four hundred dollars?

BECKY

I'll pay it back, I promise.

BOB

Jesus, Becky. I don't have that kind of dough lying around. You know I was watching PBS—

BECKY

You're always watching goddamn PBS— You'd get more customers in here if you put sports on—

BOB

I don't like sports.

BECKY

Why the hell not?

BOB

Always seemed like a goddamn waste of time, I can't afford to have my day ruined because some guy misses a foul shot. Anyway, on PBS—

BECKY

Are you going to help me, Bob?

BOB

Or was it *Planet Money?*— They said most people in this country couldn't come up with four hundred bucks in an emergency. They don't have a good friend or family member they can ask.

BECKY

That's why I'm coming to you. You're a friend who feels like family.

BOB

Really?

BECKY

Yeah.

Bob is moved.

BOB

Hm. So what's the emergency?

BECKY

Bills.

BOB

Gail?

Becky nods.
He opens the cash register. He starts counting.

You gotta pay me back though Becky.

                        BECKY

I know.

                        BOB

Or Sharon's going to notice we're coming up short.

He hands her the cash.

I only have two-fifty here. Can you make up the other one-fifty?

                        BECKY

Nope.

Bob sighs.

                        BOB

All right, I'll go to the back.

He starts to leave.

                        BECKY

Thanks, Bob.

When he's out of sight she looks around and puts the crystals in his cash register.
She shoves the register closed. It dings and she jumps.

Scene 8 — To Build a Fire.

Becky does a ritual at home. She has her phone and some kindling.

BECKY

Siri. Siri. How do you build a fire?

VOICE OF SIRI

How do you build fear?

BECKY

No. How do you build a fire?

VOICE OF SIRI

How do you build afar?

BECKY

Fuck you, Siri.

                    VOICE OF SIRI
I'm sorry, but you don't have to swear at me—

                        BECKY
How to build a fire.

                    VOICE OF SIRI
First, break kindling over your legs.

Becky does.

Next, make sure there is space between the logs. Things need air to
breathe and burn— this is true of love, God, art, and fire.

Becky looks suspicious that Siri is talking in that poetic manner.

So stack carefully, in a pyramid, with lots of space in between.

Becky does.

Now watch the fire burn.

Becky puts the witch herbs in the fire.

                        BECKY
Okay—spirits—
God, I feel dumb talking to myself.
Gail— Come home, okay? Just get better and come home.

The flames go up, up, up.

Scene 9 — Gail Comes Home.

Gail comes home from the hospital. Becky hugs her.

BECKY

I'm just so goddamn glad you're home.

GAIL

Me too.

BECKY

Come sit. Cuddle.

GAIL

I'm getting too old to cuddle.

BECKY

C'mon.

They cuddle.

I think I got two more worry lines since you've been gone.

GAIL

Sorry . . .

BECKY

It's okay. I'm glad I have wrinkles, you know why?

GAIL

Why?

BECKY

Because each wrinkle is something I did with you. These smile lines, me smiling at you. These worry lines here—me worrying about you. These lines here—me making funny faces at you when you were a baby.

Becky makes a funny face.
Gail smiles for the first time since she's been home.

GAIL

Yeah.

BECKY

So what'd they do with you at the hospital? Did your bad thoughts go away?

GAIL

I don't really want to talk about it.

BECKY

You feel better though?

GAIL

Yeah.

BECKY

You sure?

GAIL

I think so. I'm just glad to be home.

BECKY

You hungry?

GAIL

Yes, so hungry.

BECKY

I'll make you some grilled cheese?

GAIL

Yes! You home all day?

BECKY

Yeah, your first day back, of course I'm home.

GAIL

That's so nice of Shelby. She gave you the day off?

BECKY

Yup. So I'll make you some grilled cheese . . . then we could—walk around Walden Pond . . . or a movie . . . What do you want to do?

The doorbell rings.

Who could that be?

GAIL

Maybe Stan?

BECKY

Who the hell is Stan?

GAIL

A guy I met at the hospital. We were in group therapy together. He got out last week. I'm just going to run and change.

Gail runs to her room.

BECKY

Okay . . .

Becky answers the door. Stan is there, wearing black eyeliner and black nail polish.

It's you.

STAN

Huh?

BECKY

From the Marriott.

STAN

What?

BECKY

I met you at the Marriott last week.

STAN

Oh, yeah, hi.

BECKY

Hi.

STAN

I'm here to see Gail? Is she home?

BECKY

GAIL! I'm Becky Nurse, her grandma.
How old are you? Because Gail is fifteen. You look older.

STAN

I'm seventeen. Can I come in?

Gail comes back, wearing something more revealing.
Becky looks at her.

Hi, Gail.

GAIL

Hi.

STAN

I thought I'd stop by.

GAIL

Welcome to our happy home.

BECKY

Would you two *youngsters* like some grilled cheese?

STAN

No thank you. I don't eat cheese.

BECKY

Okay.

GAIL

We'll go out. Right?

STAN

Yeah.

BECKY

Out where?

STAN

For a drive?

GAIL

Sure.

BECKY

A drive with no destination? You gotta have a destination.

GAIL

Fine, we'll go to—that new café. Hungry Ghost.

STAN

Hungry Ghost it is.

BECKY

Who would name a café that?

STAN

It's a Buddhist thing.

BECKY

How many Buddhists are in Salem?

STAN

It's in Danvers.

BECKY

You're driving her outside of Salem?

GAIL

Oh my God, it's only two minutes outside town.

BECKY

Gail, you bring your phone; you text me when you get there and when you leave.

GAIL

Okay.

BECKY

And take a cardigan.

GAIL

I don't need a cardigan. It's warm out for November.

BECKY

I said take a goddamn cardigan.

Becky gives Gail her own cardigan and Gail puts it on.

GAIL

Happy?

BECKY

Not really. Bye.

GAIL AND STAN

Bye.

They leave.
Becky sits down and opens mail.
Bills, bills, bills.

BECKY

Bills, bills, bills. No reason to open the mail anymore. Just bills.

Can't someone write a goddamn thank-you note sometime? Just to break up the fucking monotony? But what would they thank you for, huh, Becky? What have you done lately that someone would thank you for?

She takes out a lighter. She burns a bill. She smokes a cigarette. If your fire chief doesn't like that, or your actress can't smoke, she tears up the bills and puts them in the garbage.

If you wish to be loved, first be lovable. That's what Mom always said.

She looks out the window for Gail. She takes a pill from her purse and swallows it. Time passes.
Gail comes home, late.
Gail comes in and takes off her cardigan.

GAIL

I texted you when I got there and when I left. Are you happy?

BECKY

I find Stan creepy. I do. That tattoo? And what's with the black nail polish?

GAIL

He helped me a lot at the hospital. He told me that I'm a good person.

BECKY

I coulda told you that.

GAIL

Then why didn't you?

BECKY

You don't believe it when your family tells you. You only believe it when some guy in black eyeliner tells you.

GAIL

Aren't you glad I made a friend?

BECKY

You need lots of friends. Not just one friend.

GAIL

Well, it's a start.

BECKY

Yes, but sometimes if you start out wrong, you don't make the right kind of friends— You know what, forget it. Let's not fight. It's your first day home. Popcorn?

GAIL

Sure.

BECKY

But are you sure he's not a Wiccan? All those Wiccans come to Salem, searching for God knows what?

47

GAIL

He's kind of into Wicca.

BECKY

Is that even allowed for guys?

GAIL

Wicca was made up by an English dude. Guys can be witches, they're, you know, wizards.

BECKY

Okay he's a *wizard*? Does he use *drugs*?

GAIL

Not anymore. He went to rehab.

BECKY

Oh, Christ. *And* he's depressed?

GAIL

Are you going to judge him for being depressed? Do you judge me for being depressed?

BECKY

No, of course not. You have reasons.

GAIL

You don't think Stan has reasons?

BECKY

I don't care about Stan. I care about you. And I don't like that Wiccan crap.

GAIL

It's not like you're Christian or anything.

BECKY

I am so Christian.

48

GAIL

Well, you don't go to church.

BECKY

Look what the church did to our ancestors.

GAIL

Exactly.

BECKY

Doesn't mean I'm not afraid of the devil.

GAIL

Oh come on, do you really believe in the devil?

BECKY

I reserve judgment.

GAIL

Cuz you're so not judgmental.

BECKY

If I was judgmental, I wouldn't have let you go on a drive with Stan. If you add an A to Stan it makes Satan, ever noticed that?

GAIL

Oh my God he's not into Satan!

BECKY

Where do his parents live?

GAIL

Portland.

BECKY

Oh, Jesus! He ran away from home? You watch out with him, you hear me? I don't want you isolating yourself with a wizard. You've been sad. I don't want a sad person to make you sadder.

GAIL

He understands my sadness.

BECKY

You need happy friends.

GAIL

I don't like cheerful adolescents.

BECKY

Wholesome friends, like your old friend Alice.

Gail groans.

She stopped by the other day. Said you should audition for the school play.

GAIL

I'm not into plays.

BECKY

Why the hell not?

GAIL

Ugh, they're doing *The Crucible* again.

BECKY

What else do they do in this goddamn town? But that's fine, that's good, you know all about the witch trials, I taught you. And you'd be with kids your own age. Maybe plays are corny, but the truth is no one is lonely while they're in a play.

GAIL

I'm not lonely when I'm with Stan.

BECKY

If I walk in on you and see you and Stan on the couch doing you know what, it would be like I walked in and found you bloody and murdered.

GAIL

Whoa. Did you just equate sex and death?

BECKY

I equated sex with Stan and death. You can have him over on the first floor only. With the door open. He's two years older than you. I don't like it.

GAIL

I'm going to my room.

BECKY

Don't shut me out, Gailie. Your mom shut me out.

GAIL

Can we not talk about Mom today?

BECKY

I'm sorry but you got a cautionary tale sitting right on top of your DNA.

GAIL

That's not helpful!

BECKY

Want to play rummy cube?

GAIL

I just need some privacy.

BECKY

Gail!

Gail exits. A door slams.

Goddammit!

Becky, alone.
Becky grabs a pill bottle from her purse but has trouble opening it and
pills spill on the ground.
Gail walks in, sees the pills.

I thought you wanted privacy.

GAIL

I need a glass of water.

BECKY

I'll get you one.

GAIL

(To the pills) What are those?

BECKY

They're for pain.

GAIL

Grandma, if you're taking pain pills, I'll fucking kill you.

BECKY

Excuse me, young lady! It's not what you think, they're for my
body. It's not like—

Gail grabs the bottle, sees the label.

GAIL

Jesus, opioids? I'm throwing these out.

BECKY

You're not in charge here, young lady. I'm in charge. Give me those.

Gail puts down the pills.

GAIL

Fine, kill yourself with pills! What do I care? I'm used to not having
a mom, my dad's dead, I can take care of myself if you die. This

whole town can rot in hell, it's like everyone's in a fucking stupor, do you know how many kids at my school have died of this shit? And for all I know, if these pills are in our house, how the hell else did Mom start? You said she was a straight-A student! Maybe it was *your* fault she died!

                    BECKY

Don't you *dare* say that to me.

                    GAIL

Sorry.

                    BECKY

Some things you can't take back.

                    GAIL

I said I was sorry.

                    BECKY

Go ahead, throw them out, I don't need them.

                    GAIL

Okay, I will.

Gail takes the pills and throws them in the garbage.
She hugs Becky, who is wooden.

Good job, Grandma.

                    BECKY

Go to your room.

Gail exits.
Becky takes the pills out of the garbage.
And takes one.

Scene 10 — I Want to Be Your Apprentice.

Becky gives the witch the four hundred dollars.
The witch starts to count it out.

BECKY

I want to apprentice with you.

WITCH

What?

BECKY

To be a witch.

WITCH

I'm not taking apprentices at this time.

BECKY

You make four hundred bucks an hour. I want to be a witch.

WITCH

I don't think you have the gift.

The witch studies Becky.

Your third eye isn't open.

BECKY

Third eye?

WITCH

(Pointing) Here.

BECKY

Yeah, it has forehead skin.

WITCH

If you want the gift of insight, you must open your third eye.

BECKY

Bullshit, my third eye is plenty open, I'm looking right at you, and what I see is that you don't want the competition. People only come see you when they're feeling desperate. And there are about four reasons to feel desperate—your kids, your money, your health, your love life—so you just run through those and see what clicks. I can do that.

WITCH

I think this session is over.

BECKY

No, I want to know. How'd you get to be a witch, did you, like, train?

WITCH

I always had the gift. It's in my blood. From a young age, I could see things. Sometimes I wish I didn't. I see that you followed my instructions about your granddaughter and she is home from the hospital now and is better. I also see that you followed my instructions and put the crystals in a cash register.

BECKY

How'd you know?

WITCH

I know. I see. I see a B—is it Bob? No, Bartender?

BECKY

Goddammit. You can see him?

WITCH

Yes, and he is a good man. I can see his aura and it is clear. That is very rare. But there is a next step for you to find love. Anoint yourself with this oil. Now, this is free.

The witch hands her the oil.
Becky groans.

First, you're going to want to mix it with a little vagina juice.

BECKY

How am I supposed to get that?

The witch just looks at her.

WITCH

You've never tasted yourself, Becky?

BECKY

No, Jesus!

WITCH

High time you did. Now, like I said, mix the oil with a little vagina juice, then put it on your neck. And go see the man you love. And put this in his room for good measure.

The witch hands Becky more crystals.

BECKY

What's in it?

WITCH

Never you mind . . . And be careful of the boy with the tattoo.

BECKY

Oh goddammit, you can see him too?

WITCH

Yes.

BECKY

He's dangerous right?

WITCH

I see—I see him changing your granddaughter's life profoundly.

BECKY

How much to get rid of him?

WITCH

Get rid of?

BECKY

I mean—make him move away. How much?

WITCH

I know you don't have much money. But you have faith. And that's worth more than money. So I'll do it reduced. Two hundred. I'll need a picture of him. See you tomorrow.

Scene 11 — Bob and Becky. At the Bar.

BOB

Becky—it's just not really sustainable. I can't keep giving you money.

BECKY

I'll work to pay you back. Can I have a job? At the bar?

BOB

It's a one-man operation.

BECKY

Did you hear that?

There is no sound.

BOB

What?

                              BECKY
I think I heard someone jiggling the lock. In the back. Bob, I think
someone's trying to break in.

                               BOB
Shit.

                              BECKY
You better go check.

Bob goes to the back.
Becky anoints herself with oil and puts a pouch of crystals in the cash
register.
Bob comes back.

                               BOB
No one was there.

                              BECKY
Oh, good.

                               BOB
Probably a racoon, or a squirrel.

Bob waters a plant.

                              BECKY
I like that you have plants at the bar. Makes it homey.

                               BOB
I like greenery. Makes the bar seem less seedy. I hate serving people
when they're too drunk. It's like feeding off people's misery. Water-
ing a plant makes me feel human again.

A moment.

                              BECKY
Remember when we went to that school dance together?

BOB

Yeah.

BECKY

And you danced with Sharon. Not with me.

BOB

Well yeah.

BECKY

So I took little pebbles from a potted palm and threw them at you while you were dancing with her.

BOB

That was you?

BECKY

Yeah, me and Nick. I told him I was mad at you for dancing with Sharon and he said, let's throw pebbles at the two of them.

BOB

That's so mean.

BECKY

Yeah, well I was jealous.

BOB

You were jealous? Sure you weren't just laughing at me? You and Nick.

BECKY

No. I wanted to dance with you. Nick said, why is your date dancing with someone else? What a dick, he said, we should throw pebbles.

Bob starts groaning and laughing.

So we did and it was kind of fun, throwing the little pebbles and then ducking so we wouldn't be seen. We sort of forgot why we were doing it because it was fun. At one point you looked up and you were like, ow, ow, that *hurt!* *(She laughs)* It just grazed your earlobe. Just about here. I felt bad then.

She touches his earlobe.

BOB

What do you smell like? A Christmas tree? A flounder? And mint? All three?

BECKY

A new shampoo.

BOB

It's kind of hot that you were jealous of me. You left that night without kissing me.

BECKY

I told you, I was mad that you danced with Sharon. Then you had to go and marry her. Jesus.

BOB

Well, I had to.

BECKY

I know. Shit, we all knew. And me—I got drunk that night—and that rock-throwing jerk took me home— The rest is history.

BOB

C'mere Becky, kiss me.

BECKY

What about Sharon?

BOB

Sharon and I—well—we don't really— We have separate beds.

BECKY

That doesn't mean she wants you to have sex with other people.

61

BOB

If she didn't want me to have sex with other people, she'd have sex with me.

BECKY

That's not always how it works in a marriage, Bob. Sometimes you just don't feel like having sex, you're not communicating to your husband, Please go have sex with someone else.

BOB

I always loved you, Becky.

BECKY

What?

BOB

You heard me.

BECKY

Then why'd you dance with Sharon?

BOB

Because she asked me to. And because I'm polite. And you know what? That's why you love me. Because I'm polite.

BECKY

I do love your politeness, Bob. Your gentleness. You're a real gentleman, Bob.

BOB

Thank you. And I'm sorry you didn't marry a gentleman and he didn't treat you right. That burned me up.

And you know what Becky? I love that you're not polite. I love that you shred all the shoulds and musts and shalls on the ground and stamp on them with your boots. I love that you're utterly, utterly yourself. Always have been.

They kiss.

Scene 12 — Sex and Death. Becky's House. Night.

Becky walks in on Stan and Gail making out on the couch.

BECKY

Aaaaagh! I told you! Out out!

They leap up.

GAIL

We weren't doing anything!

BECKY

Bullshit!

Becky throws her shoe at Stan.

STAN

Ow!

GAIL

Hey! What the—

BECKY

Now get out. But first I'm going to take your picture.

STAN

What?

BECKY

That's right. Smile, Wiccan!

Becky takes a picture of him.

GAIL

What is *wrong* with you?— Jesus! I'm going to Stan's! Stan, can you drive us to Gloucester?

STAN

Sure.

BECKY

Young lady, you are staying right here in this house! Gail!

Stan and Gail leave.

Get back here!

Becky throws her other shoe after them.

I will ground you so hard! Goddammit—young lady, you are not going to Gloucester!

But they are gone.
Becky picks up her shoes.
She feels a pain when bending down.

Ow.
Goddammit.

She grabs a pill bottle.
And takes a pill.

Scene 13 — He Wears Black Eyeliner.

Becky at the witch.

BECKY

Here's the two hundred dollars. And his picture. *(Showing her a picture on her phone)* He wears black eyeliner, see?

WITCH

Right. *(She looks at Stan's picture and frowns)* Hm. He looks familiar. I think he came to me once.

BECKY

Yeah, that's how I got your number.

WITCH

Hmm . . . That's not really ethical—because he was a client . . . hmm . . .

BECKY
Fine, I'll take my two hundred dollars back.

WITCH
No, no. I'll find a way to balance it out somehow. I don't do dark
magic, but I can encourage flight. Here. Put this charm in his bag.

The witch gives Becky a charm.

BECKY
How the hell am I supposed to do that? He's shacking up with Gail
in Gloucester.

WITCH
Does he have a workplace?

BECKY
Yeah. The Marriott. Okay.

WITCH
Good. And well-done on the love potion. I can see it was a success.

BECKY
How can you see?

WITCH
I see the love on you, all over you, it's in your aura, I hate that word
but there it is. Your aura is glowing. It's rosy—slightly pink.

BECKY
Wow. Here's the thing. I still don't have a job.

WITCH
Yes. I've been thinking about that. Your old boss?

BECKY
Shelby.

WITCH

Yes. I think you need to remove the bad energy she's created in your life. Burn this incense and put the ashes into a little pile in her desk. And sprinkle some of this holy water around her desk to protect yourself from her. And if there's anything in the museum that could be helpful to remove the Nurse curse—an object—a statue? Bring it to me. Come back Friday to tell me how it goes.

BECKY

No, I can't afford to come back here. Every time I come back, I have to pay you more money.

WITCH

Look, Becky. I like you. I have to pay rent, like anyone else, plus my landlord wants to kick me out and put in a Starbucks. Otherwise I would do this for free. But at the end of the day, none of this is about money. You don't really want anything material. No one does. You want hope for your granddaughter, you want health, you want love. Is this true?

Becky nods.

And you're in pain, no? What is it? Down below?

BECKY

I hate when you do that. Fine. Endometriosis. Childbirth for me was like a wound that never quite closed up. I bled, and bled, and bled. They took my uterus out.

WITCH

But you still have pain, am I right?

BECKY

Yeah.

WITCH

Can I touch?

67

BECKY

Okay.

The witch feels around Becky's midsection, hovering her hand over the area.

WITCH

You can't be taking pain pills for this. I'll make you an herbal remedy. Women have used it for centuries . . . Wait wait . . . oh . . .

BECKY

What is it? Am I dying?

WITCH

No, no.
Hold on a second.
Shh.
Shh.

The witch sees something invisible.

I think I see your daughter.

BECKY

What?

WITCH

She wants to say something to you.
She says: Sorry, Mom. She says: I couldn't help it, Mom.

BECKY

Tell her: Thank you.

WITCH

You can tell her directly.

BECKY

Can she hear me?

The witch nods.

WITCH

Tell her anything you want.

BECKY

(To the air) Hi—hi, Amy?
(To the witch) I don't like to talk about my feelings.

WITCH

I know you don't Becky. But she's listening. She's here—

BECKY

Amy? I'll never get over your leaving us, you know that? And do you know how mad I am at you? Do you know that the sad is so big and the mad is so big sometimes they cancel each other out and all I am is numb and I can't feel a fucking thing?

The witch bows her head. Her head comes back up, and she becomes Amy.

WITCH AS AMY

I know you have great anger, Mom. There is no anger where I am. There's no pain here.
God is the pill.
Thank you for taking care of Gail.
Beware the eyes lit up in the dark.

The witch comes back to herself.

WITCH

She left. Sorry—I'm exhausted. I need to sleep now. Don't forget— crystals in the backpack, incense and holy water on your boss's desk. See you next week.

Scene 14—Becky Runs into Herself in the Dark.

Becky sneaks around in the dark with her flashlight.
She sticks a charm into the Marriott desk.
Then she sneaks into the museum.
She bumps into Shelby's desk.

BECKY

Goddammit.

She puts ashes and holy water around the desk.
She sees the Rebecca Nurse statue with glowing eyes.

Let's go.

Becky takes the statue.
And runs out.

Scene 15 — Toast Is Better When Someone Else Makes It for You.

Becky putting on a Rebecca Nurse costume.
Next to her is the statue of Rebecca Nurse.
A poster board next to her, and some markers.
Bob enters in his underwear.

BOB

What's that costume for?

BECKY

I'm gonna start my own Salem tours. Like *The Real* Salem Tour, conducted by a *Real Live* descendent of Rebecca Nurse. I'll show all the real spots—like the jail where the witches were locked up, which is now the Verizon store. I can't depend on you for money anymore, Bob. It's not right.

How do I look?

BOB

Like a sexy Pilgrim.

BECKY

Why, thank you.

BOB

Did you hear Shelby fell and broke her hip and is on leave for a month?

BECKY

What?

BOB

Yeah, I ran into Donna at the post office who heard.

BECKY

How'd she fall?

BOB

She said it was the damndest thing. Just slipped on a little water. Right near her desk.

Becky does the sign of the cross.

Maybe you could replace her—

BECKY

No!

BOB

Why not? You were always the smartest girl at St. Mary, Star of the Sea—won the third grade spelling bee . . .

BECKY

That's true, I did.

BOB

Got me out on the word "principal."

BECKY

It's not my fault, you spelled it super goddamn weird.

BOB

I was spelling principle as in virtue—

BECKY

'Course you were—

BOB

Dance with me.

BECKY

What?

BOB

I'm so happy. Dance with me. Moon river . . . da da da da da . . . da da da da da da da . . .

They dance a little. The door opens. In walks Gail, weeping.

BECKY

Gail, baby, what's wrong?

GAIL

Stan's gone! He left! He broke up with me!

BECKY

Oh, honey. Why?

GAIL

He said he couldn't explain—that we weren't really in love—and I said what are you talking about, I love you! And then he fled! Like literally ran off into the night!

BECKY

I'm so sorry. Oh, honey, come here. Sit on my lap.

GAIL

I'm too old to—

BECKY

Aw, sit on my lap.

Gail sits on her grandma's lap.
Becky bounces her up and down like a child and Gail slowly stops crying.

GAIL

What's Bob doing here?

BOB

Just making toast.

GAIL

Why are you making toast in your underwear?

BECKY

Bob and I are old high school friends, you know.

BOB

I'm gonna get going now.

BECKY

Gail. The first man isn't usually the right man. It's like a pancake. You heat up the griddle and you burn the first pancake. Or it's half-done, with a little runny batter in the middle. Your third or fourth pancake is good. My mother always said it's like having children. The first time around, you might not get it right.

GAIL

But Mom was your only.

BECKY

Yes.

GAIL

And I'm my mother's first and only.

BECKY

Yes. What I meant is you're my second-chance pancake, Gail. Grandmas flip pancakes better than moms. They watch more and less closely. They know how to do that. Hold you close but not too close.

Gail is sad.

BOB

Can I make you some cinnamon toast, Gail?

GAIL

That would be nice.

BOB

You like lots of butter?

GAIL

Sure.

BOB

It's funny but toast always tastes better when someone else makes it for you.

That makes Gail even sadder.
He butters some toast.

BECKY

Now Gail, you're a smart young lady with a good head on your shoulders. I didn't want to say so at the time because you seemed to enjoy his company, but Stan was trouble, Gail.

GAIL

I'm going to my room.

BOB

Don't forget your toast.

He gives her the toast.

GAIL

Thanks.

75

Gail exits.

BECKY

Thank God.

BOB

You know what that's code for? When a teenage guy says: "We're not really in love"? Means she wouldn't do it with him.

BECKY

How would you know?

BOB

I know. But we, on the other hand—weren't we in the middle of something?

He pulls her up.

BECKY

I can't, Gail's upstairs . . .

BOB

Aw c'mon.

They dance.

BECKY

Maybe my luck is turning around. I'm going to pay you back, Bob. Every cent.

BOB

I don't want your money, darling. I just want your body. Your smoking hot sixty-two-year-old body. *(Or whatever age the actress is or wants to be)* I want it, I want it, I think about you all the time. What have you done to me, Becky? It's like you've bewitched me, enchanted me.

She looks at him suddenly.

What's wrong?

BECKY

Bob, I have a confession to make.

BOB

What—you have a venereal disease?

BECKY

Jesus! Do you think so badly of me?

BOB

No! It's just—confessions aren't usually about good deeds.

BECKY

Maybe you oughta sit down.
Okay. So—I saw a witch.

BOB

What?

BECKY

I bought our love from a witch. I even used your money. I've been feeling so guilty about it.

BOB

I don't understand.

BECKY

I wanted to be honest with you. Because I'm having feelings for you, Bob. Like, the kind I haven't had in years. The kind that makes me want to pick a flower and put it in my hair. But I'm worried that our love is based on a lie. I put crystals in your drawer. And anointed myself with—oil. Bob, you're—enchanted.

BOB

I'm sort of touched you did a love spell on me actually.

BECKY

Really?

BOB

Yeah, it means you wanted me . . . cared enough to put crystals in
my drawer.
Kiss me, Becky. Better yet, marry me.

BECKY

What? You're already married. That's the enchantment talking.

BOB

I'll get a divorce.

BECKY

First, I want to prove that we're really in love and it's not the
enchantment.

BOB

How do we do that?

BECKY

We can have sex while I'm not wearing the love potion.

BOB

Great! I love having sex with you.

BECKY

Not now, Gail's upstairs . . .

BOB

She's not coming down, c'mon . . . you got me all riled up . . .

BECKY

Okay, but first, let me scrub off the love potion. Hold on . . .

She finds a wet one. She wipes the potion off her neck.
Bob starts to disrobe. He starts kissing her.

BOB

You smell like wet ones.

BECKY

You still want me even though I smell like a baby, or an old people's home, or an airplane?

BOB

All of those thoughts are so very unsexy and yet *this*— *(Indicating an erection)* upright glory—is proof positive of my deep and abiding love for you.

They make out. They get more and more passionate.

BECKY

Oh Bob. Oh Bob—Bob, can I call you something other than Bob? A secret name? Like Robbie—or do you like Bobbie?

BOB

Call me Raphael.

BECKY

Raphael?

BOB

It's my middle name.

BECKY

How did I not know that?

BOB

My mom was big into angels.

BECKY

Oh, kiss me, Raphael. And call me Rebecca!

They kiss.

BOB

Rebecca—

                        BECKY

Raphael—

                        BOB

Rebecca—

                        BECKY

Raphael—

                        BOB

Oh—

                        BECKY

Oh—

                        BOB

Oh—no—wait a second—

                        BECKY

What?

                        BOB

Hold on—

                        BECKY

What?

                        BOB

I feel a little weird.

                        BECKY

You okay?

                        BOB

I think it's—

                        BECKY

You want me to—

BOB

No—I think it's my heart—call Sharon—

BECKY

I can't call *Sharon*—

BOB

Call an ambulance—Becky— *(As he falls)*

BECKY

Bob!

Scene 16 — Bob's Heart. At the Hospital.

Bob in a hospital bed with an aura of light around him.
Becky at his side.

BOB

And then I saw the Virgin Mary. And she told me I was descended from John Proctor. And that my soul is virtuous. And that I should go by my middle name from the archangel Raphael, until my illness passes me over.

BECKY

Uh-huh.

BOB

She also said Bob was a bad name, a palindrome with a hole in the center of it like a donut. And there's a hole in history like a hole in a donut, with blood in that hole. And that I had to stop serving liquor at a bar. Because liquor degrades the amount of numinous spirit in the world. So I'm selling the bar.

BECKY

Okay, sell the bar, that's fine. I'm just so goddamn glad you're alive.

BOB

(With joy) I'm alive! And also—

BECKY

What is it?

BOB

The Virgin Mary told me I'm a man of principle, and that's why I spelled principal the way I did in the spelling bee.

BECKY

Okay, Bob, whatever you say.

BOB

Well, the thing is—

BECKY

Yeah—

BOB

She also reminded me that I'm married. And I need to stay true to my wife. And she said if I do all that, I could live.

BECKY

What are you saying?

BOB

I'm just telling you what she said.

BECKY

But are you going to *do* what she said?

BOB

Becky, I'm confused. One minute I'm in my body, the next I'm not, now I'm here, and I have all these instructions from the Virgin Mary.

BECKY

Bob—you hated all that Catholic school crap growing up.

BOB

Raphael.

BECKY

The witch was right. I couldn't tell anyone. Not even you.

BOB

The spells—the crystals—come on, I *almost died of a heart attack*! Becky, you might not understand because you've never had a near-death experience—but I'm being given a second chance.

BECKY

Yeah, I thought *you* were my second chance, Bob.

BOB

I'm sorry. Sharon will be here any minute.

BECKY

Well give my regards to Sharon. Jesus.

BOB

Becky—don't be like that—

BECKY

Goodbye, Bob.

Becky exits.

Scene 17—Lock Her Up. The Town Square.

Becky behind a placard that reads: THE REAL TOUR OF SALEM.
She stands next to the statue of Rebecca Nurse.
She is wearing her Pilgrim costume.

BECKY

Now. Here we stand on the *real* site of Gallows Hill, where John Proctor was hung. You don't know about John Proctor? None of you read *The Crucible*? Well, John Proctor was a man of principle. *The Crucible* is the story of one virtuous man but in real life, Salem is the story of fourteen dead women. When I got to thinking about that, it kind of irritated me.

You know, when Arthur Miller was writing *The Crucible*, he was married to another woman, but he really wanted to fuck Marilyn Monroe who was much younger. He was like—I want to fuck her, but I can't fuck her. And so he wrote a play about it.

And now our country's whole understanding of the Salem witch trials is based on the feeling of—I want to fuck Marilyn Monroe, but I can't fuck her! And that's *really weird* when you think about it.

So . . . should we have a moment of silence for the so-called witches who were put to death beneath the hallowed ground of this Dunkin's? What? You want to get a coffee first? Okay, okay, that's fine, I'll do the silence for you.

She bows her head in silence for a moment.
The jailer, a police officer, appears.

Can I help you?

JAILER

Hey, Becky.

BECKY

Hey, Officer Friendly.

JAILER

Do you have a license to give tours on a public street?

BECKY

You need a license to give tours?

JAILER

Yes indeed-y.

BECKY

I gave tours at the museum all the time.

JAILER

You were employed there. That's different. Becky, I'm sorry to have to do this, I know you've had a bad time of it, but there's footage of you entering the museum at night.

BECKY

Oh fuck.

JAILER

And I believe you have a statue that belongs to the museum.

BECKY

It belongs to the descendants of Rebecca Nurse.

JAILER

Not according to the museum.

The jailer grabs the statue.

BECKY

No, it's my goddamn statue!

JAILER

I'm going to have to take you in.

BECKY

Oh no you're not.

He puts his hand on her and she struggles.

JAILER

If you're gonna be that way, Becky, I gotta cuff you.

BECKY

Stop it, stop it! You ought to rot in hell for keeping a woman from making an honest living!

They bizarrely go back in time.
The jailer changes his voice to an old-timey voice and becomes a magistrate.
The witch, Stan, Shelby, Bob and Gail enter in Pilgrim attire.
Becky becomes Rebecca Nurse.

MAGISTRATE

Woman, thou hast cursed an officer of the law! 'Tis witchcraft!

CROWD

Lock her up!

REBECCA NURSE

You canst not lock up an old woman!

CROWD

Lock her up!

MAGISTRATE

This woman is a witch. Confess! Confess!

They all point their fingers at Rebecca Nurse.

CROWD

Lock her up!

REBECCA NURSE

I will not confess!
You are a liar!

CROWD

Lock her up!

REBECCA NURSE

I am no more witch than you are wizard! And if you take away my
life, God will give you blood to drink!

A large crowd chants:

CROWD

LOCK HER UP LOCK HER UP!
LOCK HER UP LOCK HER UP!
KILL THE WITCH LOCK HER UP!

ACT TWO

Scene 1

Becky, as Rebecca Nurse, still in the town square in a Pilgrim outfit, shackled.

MAGISTRATE

Woman, thou hast cursed an officer of the law! 'Tis witchcraft!

REBECCA NURSE

You canst not lock up an old woman!

CROWD

Lock her up!

MAGISTRATE

This woman is a witch. Confess! Confess!

They all point their fingers at Rebecca Nurse.

CROWD

Lock her up!

REBECCA NURSE

I will not confess! You are a liar!

CROWD

Lock her up!
KILL THE WITCH LOCK HER UP!

REBECCA NURSE

I am no more witch than you are wizard! And if you take away my life, God will give you blood to drink!

MAGISTRATE

You would do well to confess and give glory to God!

CROWD

Lock her up! Lock her up! Lock her up!

REBECCA NURSE

I am as clear as the child unborn!

We hear a large crowd, from rallies contemporary and ancient, chanting:

CROWD

LOCK HER UP LOCK HER UP LOCK HER UP!

The magistrate comes toward Rebecca Nurse.
Suddenly, Becky wakes up in a jail cell, yelling.
The magistrate is now the jailer.

JAILER

Becky, stop screaming, I'm not, like, torturing you.

BECKY

Where am I?

JAILER

You're in jail for breaking and entering.

BECKY

Oh. Don't I get a phone call?

JAILER

I hope you're calling a lawyer.

He gives her a phone. Becky makes a phone call.

BECKY

Gail, it's me, I'm so sorry. I'm in jail. For what? For nothing. A lawyer? They'll probably give me some court-appointed yahoo. Look,
keep the door locked at night. I should be home soon. Love you.

She hangs up.

Goddammit.

He goes through her purse.
Finds her medicine.

JAILER

What are these?

He looks more closely, sees they're opioids.

Ah . . . You can't have these in jail.

BECKY

Those are doctor's prescriptions. I have chronic pain.

JAILER

Don't we all?

BECKY

No. Some of us are in more pain than others.

91

JAILER

Hard to prove.

BECKY

How long are you going to keep me in this jail without my prescription medication?

JAILER

That's up to the judge. People crush this up and snort this stuff.

BECKY

I'm a grandma for Chrissakes, do I look like a junkie?

JAILER

Being a junkie is a real equal-opportunity deal. What am I going to do with these?

BECKY

Just throw 'em out. I don't need them.

JAILER

Okey-doke.

BECKY

Can I get an Advil?

JAILER

I'll put in a request.
Afraid I gotta lock you up now.
Sorry, Becky.

Scene 2 — Bob Visits Becky in Jail.

JAILER

You have a visitor.

Becky sits up.

BECKY

Bob!

BOB

I brought you a book.

He hands her a Bible.

BECKY

You know, funnily enough, a Bible is the one book they already have in jail. How's your heart?

BOB

It's ticking. I was in the pharmacy, picking up my heart medication, and I heard you were in jail. Becky, why do you always shoot yourself in the foot?

BECKY

Maybe it's a curse, from my past.

BOB

I don't believe in curses.

BECKY

Maybe cuz you're not cursed.

BOB

You're not cursed, Becky, you just—you do these things . . .

BECKY

All I was doing was trying to earn a living.

BOB

I heard you broke into the museum?

BECKY

Well, yeah.

BOB

I mean, Becky—

BECKY

Sure, it was dumb—but here I am.

BOB

Becky—I've been doing a great deal of reflection. I'm selling the bar. And when I get my strength back, I'm going back to school to become a history teacher—

BECKY

Well, that's great, Bob. Really.

BOB

Sharon's very supportive.

BECKY

Well, good for Sharon. You can go now.

BOB

Come on. I want to help you. Like—as a friend, or a Good Samaritan.

BECKY

You're still on the Virgin Mary stuff?

BOB

It's not "stuff." It was an epiphany. I wanna help you, Becky.

BECKY

Actually, I have a favor to ask you.
I need to make bail so I can go home and take care of Gail.

BOB

How much is bail?

BECKY

Two thousand dollars.

BOB

Jesus, Becky!!!!

BECKY

You said you were selling the bar . . . If I show up for my trial, which
I will, you'll get the money back, it's a loan.

BOB

What would Sharon say?

BECKY

Why do you have to tell Sharon?

BOB

I tell her everything now. So I can't bail you out.

BECKY

Okay, then.

BOB

Is there something else I can bring you? Like: soup?

BECKY

Actually, yes. The guard took away my medicine. Maybe you could pick it up for me at home or I have another script at the CVS.

BOB

Is that allowed?

BECKY

I think so.

BOB

I'll see what I can do.

BECKY

What would Christ do?

BOB

Are you really going to bring him into this?

BECKY

Isn't he always present? Not like you have to "bring him in."

BOB

Don't be bitter.

BECKY

You used to like my bitter.

JAILER

(Over the loudspeaker) Visiting time is over.

BECKY

Are you or are you not a Good Samaritan, Bob?

BOB

I'll pray on it.

Bob leaves.
Becky, alone.
She feels a little weird. Woozy.
She sits on the toilet.
Time passes.

BECKY

(To the jailer) Hey! Did you put in a request for my medicine?

JAILER

Denied.

Scene 3 — Gail Visits Becky.

Gail enters. She is dressed as a Pilgrim.

JAILER

You have another visitor.

BECKY

Gail! I'm sorry you have to see me here.

GAIL

Uh, yeah. It's pretty fucked up, Grandma.

BECKY

It's a travesty of justice is what it is.

GAIL

Right.

BECKY

Why are you dressed like a Pilgrim?

GAIL

Why are *you* dressed like a Pilgrim?

BECKY

You first.

GAIL

I got into the school play.

BECKY

You did???

GAIL

Yes. They gave us our costumes today.

BECKY

Oh Gail! That's great. Who are you playing?

GAIL

Betty. She doesn't have many lines but that's good because it's less to memorize. I just have to twitch and have spasms and stare into space. And I told the other girls about how real-life Abigail was actually eleven and probably never even met John Proctor.

So whenever John Proctor calls her a whore, we all shout from the wings: "No, you're the whore, John Proctor, you're the whore."

BECKY

I'm so glad you're getting involved with wholesome school activities.

GAIL

Yeah. I wrote an epilogue too.

BECKY

You did? Let's hear it.

GAIL

Something like: "Every time another woman takes a bow in *The Crucible*, another lie is told about how the lust of young women destroys good men."

BECKY

Wow! I can't wait to see it.

GAIL

Hopefully you'll be out of *jail*.

BECKY

I will. I promise. Any day now.

GAIL

The director's a little creepy.

BECKY

What do you mean?

GAIL

He said the girls should dance naked in the forest—to "feel our backstory."

BECKY

With him?

GAIL

No, with each other. I guess he's just out of the seminary? And he said we should take pictures for our character journals.

BECKY

Jesus Christ, I'm calling the school.

GAIL

Stan said—

BECKY

Stan? Is he in touch with you?

GAIL

Oh, he's living with me.

BECKY

What? No!

GAIL

I was kind of scared to stay alone at night. So I called Stan and he came right over.

BECKY

Jesus. No—young lady, you *cannot* be living with a man, you're way too young.

GAIL

Look—Stan cooks. He takes care of me. He's even been teaching me about Wicca—

BECKY

No, no, no—

GAIL

What are you going to do about it? You're in jail.

BECKY

Unacceptable!

GAIL

If you're going to yell at me, I'll just leave.

BECKY

No, no, don't leave. Listen. What are you two doing for money?

GAIL

Stan's got the Marriott, and I got a job interview: Heaven's Maid— freelance grave tending and flower delivery. Twenty-one bucks an hour, just for gardening. I visit Mom's grave enough, might as well get paid for it.

BECKY

Twenty-one bucks an hour is great. Does it require experience?

GAIL

Yeah, but Stan used to live on a hydroponic gardening collective in Vermont? So he's going to teach me. You're supposed to be eighteen, but I can look eighteen, I think. I just turned sixteen, anyway.

BECKY

Oh! Happy Birthday! I'm so sorry I was in jail for your birthday. Happy Birthday, sweet girl.

GAIL

(Starts to cry) I feel so alone . . . I've got no one, nothing, if it weren't for Stan . . .

BECKY

Honey, no . . .

GAIL

Stan made me a three-layer cake for my birthday. But there was no one but us to eat it. He didn't want to invite any of my friends. He says they're immature.

BECKY

Well, they are *younger* than him.

GAIL

He says I'm more mature than my friends. Because I've suffered. And then he quotes the Bible. *(Gail picks up the Bible)* "He who increaseth in knowledge increaseth in sorrow." Stan says that's why we get along. Because we're smarter than other people because we're sadder than other people.

BECKY

No, the Bible isn't saying being depressed makes you smart, it says the more you know the more depressed you get.

GAIL

Stan says—

BECKY

It's bullshit, Gail. I want you to be happy. That is the wish of mothers and grandmothers for their children. Even if we ourselves are not happy, even if deep down we're not sure if happiness even exists, still we have this dumb certain hope that happiness will and must exist for our children, for our grandchildren, and if we cannot provide that for them—well, then we are the worst fucking failures on this planet.

JAILER

(Over the loudspeaker) Visiting time is over.

BECKY

Bye, Gail.

GAIL

Bye, Grandma.

They hug.

I'm scared.

BECKY

Of what?

GAIL

When I pretend to be Betty, and twitch and shake, it's like I'm not in my body, and I think of Mom, and then Betty has to scream for her dead mother, and I scream that I'm flying to her—and suddenly I'm not pretending at all—and I worry I'm going to end up like Mom somehow—

BECKY

No. You're not going to end up like her. You're different.

JAILER

(Over the loudspeaker) Okey-doke.

GAIL

Maybe I should go back to the hospital while you're in jail?

BECKY

We can't afford the hospital. And I'll be out any day. Just sit tight, okay?

JAILER

(Over the loudspeaker) Come on now.

Scene 4 — You Have a New Roommate.

Night.
Becky, alone.
She feels a little woozy, chills.
A sudden light goes on overhead.

JAILER
(Over the loudspeaker) You have a new roommate, Becky.

The witch enters.

BECKY

You.

WITCH

Hello, Becky.

BECKY

You ruined my life. I'm in jail, I went and lost Bob, and my grand-daughter's living with a Wiccan—all since I saw you.

WITCH

That was your own free will, Becky. You lost Bob because you told him about the love ointment.

BECKY

Could you just shut your third eye? Just shut it?

WITCH

Do you want me to bring Bob back to you?

BECKY

No. If he comes back to me, I want him to come of his own free will. I should never have come to see you. This is all your fault.

WITCH

It's dangerous to change the laws of the universe with witchcraft. It doesn't always go the way we plan, and it's not like witches have malpractice insurance.

BECKY

I want my money back. That was extortion, manipulation, fraud, of course I wanted to talk to my daughter.

WITCH

What could be worth more than talking to your child?

BECKY

That wasn't her. You're a fake. That's why you're here, isn't it?

WITCH

No. I'm here because I was at a protest with activist witches doing a hex on the president in a public square.

                        BECKY

Everything you said was generic as fuck. I forgive you, Mom, thank
you, Mom.

                        WITCH

Forgiveness is never generic.

Becky is in pain.
The witch puts a hand on Becky's abdomen.

I told you to stop using those pain pills and use an herbal remedy.
You got the shakes, Becky? The chills? The runs?

                        BECKY

I'm *fine.*

                        WITCH

But you're seeing things? Ah—your third eye is open!

The witch puts her hand on Becky's forehead.

                        BECKY

Teach me how to shut it.

                        WITCH

Once it is open you cannot shut it. The veil is thin.

                        BECKY

How much have I paid you at this point? Two thousand dollars?
I want my money back!!!!!!!

                        WITCH

I no longer have the money.

                        BECKY

That's my bail!!! And I need to go home!

                        WITCH

Becky, calm down.

BECKY

I won't calm down! Give me the money! Give me my money, you fucking witch!

Becky goes at her.
The witch restrains her.

WITCH

Yes. That's right. I am a witch.
But not the kind of witch you're talking about.
There are witches and there are witches and I am a WITCH.
That cheap psychic you saw—she was not a real witch.

BECKY

But you—you are that cheap psychic.

WITCH

No.

BECKY

No?

WITCH

No.
I am a healer. She was a stealer.

BECKY

Why are you *rhyming?*

WITCH

I rhyme because of time, time, time.
I join what must be joined
and sever what must be severed.
And I have been here forever.
I can talk to the moon and the loon and the wind—
Now let me in, let me in, let me in—

BECKY

No, no—

WITCH

Do you know how I know that Rebecca Nurse was innocent of witchcraft?

BECKY

How?

WITCH

If she were a real witch, she would have escaped.
I told you I would remove the Nurse curse.
But how can I do that from here?
Have ya read the *transcripts*, Becky?
I'm going through the pinhole of history, Becky.
And you're coming with me.

The witch closes her eyes and mutters.
The lights do something weird.
She disappears.

Scene 5 — Becky Falls through a Hole in History.

The jailer now has on a magistrate's wig and robes.
The rest of the cast enters in Pilgrim costumes.
Becky, as Rebecca Nurse, is handcuffed.
The following is taken from actual transcripts of the trial of Rebecca Nurse.

MAGISTRATE
Are you innocent of this witchcraft?

REBECCA NURSE AND WITCH
I can say before my Eternal Father that I am innocent and God will clear my innocency.

ABIGAIL
(Played by Gail) She's pinching me! She's pinching me!

REBECCA NURSE AND WITCH
The Lord knows I have not hurt them!

MAGISTRATE
Have you familiarity with spirits?

REBECCA NURSE AND WITCH
None but with God alone.

MAGISTRATE
You have been known to differ with your neighbors—

REBECCA NURSE AND WITCH
Who has not?

MAGISTRATE
Concerning a pig in your garden—

AN ANGRY PILGRIM
(Played by Shelby) My pigs got into your corn—and you cursed us—

REBECCA NURSE
Your fence had a hole in it—

AN ANGRY PILGRIM
You entreated your husband to KILL our pigs—but he would not—
so instead—you cursed my husband— He went blind and died—

REBECCA NURSE
I have got nobody to look to but God.

MAGISTRATE
These girls accuse you of hurting them. And if you think it is
not unwittingly but by design, then you must look upon them as
murderers.

REBECCA NURSE AND WITCH
I cannot hear you, I am an old woman and hard of hearing.

Rebecca Nurse shakes her head.
Abigail imitates the head shaking.

MAGISTRATE

Do you look upon these young women as murderers?

REBECCA NURSE

I cannot help it, if the devil may appear in my shape.

MAGISTRATE

So then you admit that the devil is using your shape.

ABIGAIL

Look! A bird does fly about her!

AN ANGRY PILGRIM

Her specter grievously tortured the girls—pinching and almost choking them to death—

REBECCA NURSE

I never afflicted no child in my life.

She leans over sick.
All the girls lean over, as though sick.

MAGISTRATE

How came you sick?

REBECCA NURSE

I am sick at my stomach.

MAGISTRATE

Do you think these girls suffer voluntary or involuntary?

REBECCA NURSE

I cannot tell.

MAGISTRATE

That is strange, everyone can judge.

REBECCA NURSE

I must be silent.

MAGISTRATE
Have you no wounds?

REBECCA NURSE
None but old age.

MAGISTRATE
Examine her for witch's marks . . .

REBECCA NURSE
What sin God found in me unrepented of, that he should cause such an affliction on me in my old age.

Rebecca Nurse is roughly handled.

Please— only a trained midwife might examine me—

They put her on the floor, hold her down, and examine her.

AN ANGRY PILGRIM
Aha! A witch's teat between her pudenda and her anus!

REBECCA NURSE
Please—I have borne eight children, magistrate—it was an injury of childbirth such as any woman might bear and any midwife would recognize.

MAGISTRATE
This woman is a witch, sure!

REBECCA NURSE
You do not know my heart.

MAGISTRATE
What have you to say in your defense?

An awful silence. Rebecca Nurse didn't hear the question.

What have you to say in your defense?

She says nothing.

Then your silence condemns you!

Becky is suddenly on a cot sleeping, and sleep talking.
The jailer approaches Becky.

BECKY

(Mumbling) I fell through a pinhole in history it was shaped like a
donut there was blood in that hole—haunted—no not that kind of
possession—*possession*—fuck you Mr. Jailer, following me around
for three hundred years—there were no women on that jury—

JAILER

(Overlapping) Becky. Wake up. You're talking in your sleep it's
freaking me out.
Becky.

Becky opens her eyes.

BECKY

Oh. It's you. Are you going to put me to death?

JAILER

For breaking and entering? No, not in the state of Massachusetts.

BECKY

Oh, good. Good. Did I get a new roommate?

JAILER

Uh, no, but you got another visitor. You're like Miss freaking Pop-
ularity. Hey, Bob.

BOB

Hey.

Scene 6 — Bob Visits Becky Again.

Bob enters.

BECKY

You came back! Of your own free will!

BOB

What are you talking about, Becky?

BECKY

(Rattled) I had a dream—or—uh—a visitation—and I *was* Rebecca Nurse. But at the most crucial moment in my trial, I kept silent, it was so awful.

BOB

That sounds scary, Becky.

BECKY

It was.

BOB

Hey, hey, listen—I brought your medicine.

BECKY

Oh God, thank you so much, I feel like shit.

He reaches into his pocket to give her the medicine.

Wait—I don't think you can just hand that to me in plain sight.

BOB

Why not?

BECKY

I'm not technically supposed to have medicine in here.

BOB

Is it legal, or not legal? What's in there, Becky?

BECKY

You didn't look?

BOB

No, I'm a gentleman.

BECKY

They're for pain.

BOB

I didn't know you were on pain meds. Like—opioids?

Becky nods.

For what?

BECKY

Lady stuff.

BOB

Oh . . .

BECKY

I just take one a day, for pain. *(He stares at her)* I was *prescribed these* by my gynecologist, okay? And I'm very careful with them.

BOB

It's just unfortunate that you're asking me to give you a controlled substance, in a jail cell.

BECKY

Could you, like, stick 'em in a muffin or something?

BOB

I don't have a muffin, Becky.

BECKY

You know what, just forget about it, Bob. I can tolerate pain. What I can't tolerate is being without you—

BOB

Becky—I'm a married man. So, look, I'm just going to give you these—and then I'm going to leave, okay? And then that's it, that's it between us. Sharon doesn't want me to see you ever again. So, I'm going to give you one last hug, and then you're going to check your pockets, because there might be something inside, *to help you with your pain.* Okay, I'm going to give you a hug now. One Last Hug.

Bob hugs Becky goodbye and awkwardly tries to find her back pocket.

BECKY

I know you don't love Sharon. You love me. As more than a Christian.

BOB

Where's your goddamn pocket?

He's trying to stuff the pills into her costume.

BECKY

I don't know if it has pockets, it's a *Pilgrim* outfit for Chrissakes, they didn't have pockets.

And the pill bottle falls on the floor.

JAILER

Becky Nurse?

The jailer approaches and picks up the pills.

Okay. Bob—I'm gonna pretend I didn't see that, because you've always been, in this town, known as an all-around good guy. And Sharon's my second cousin. As you know. And I have a feeling this one put you up to it. Now, get on home to your wife, Bob. *(To Becky)* As for you, possession—not good. Now get back in there.

The jailer puts the pills in his pocket.
The sound of a clink.

Scene 7 — Sign Our Book. And Shelby.

Becky is alone.
She feels weird.
Sweaty.
Nauseous.

MANY VOICES

(Whispering, overlapping) Becky Nurse, we found you, sign our book . . .

BECKY

I won't!

MANY VOICES

(Shelby, the witch, Stan, the jailer, Gail; whispering, overlapping) Becky Nurse, dance with us . . .

BECKY

No, I won't, I won't!

MANY VOICES

Drink from our cup!

OTHER VOICES

'Tis spectral evidence against you!!

BECKY

No!

From the jailer's radio, we hear fragments of commentators talking about Trump and witch hunts.

(Shouting at the jailer) Can you turn that shit off?

JAILER

You think you get to have an opinion on programming in here?

BECKY

It's giving me a headache.

JAILER

You're giving me a headache.

BECKY

Witch hunt this and witch hunt that—what a bunch of bullshit. You can't keep me in here forever. When the hell is my court date?

JAILER

The court's backed up. And the irony is, for breaking and entering, you'd be talking ten months, but for trying to smuggle drugs in, we're talking two years.

BECKY

No, no, no, no, I gotta get home to my granddaughter.

JAILER

That's up to the judge, not me. You got a visitor.
But, Becky, I'm watching you like a hawk. No funny business.

Shelby enters on crutches.

SHELBY

I didn't want you to go to jail. I just didn't want you breaking into my desk.

BECKY

Well, here I am.

SHELBY

Also, you were spreading misinformation. In this day and age, it's important to get your facts right. Gallows Hill *was not at the Dunkin' Donuts*. It's near the Walgreens. We're putting up a plaque this year for the 325th anniversary.

BECKY

No, Shelby, it's at the Dunkin' Donuts.

SHELBY

Walgreens.

BECKY

Dunkin's! Believe your Harvard fuckwads if you want. Anyway, what the hell are you doing here?

SHELBY

I came to discuss something with you. Can I sit?

BECKY

Be my guest.

Becky gestures and Shelby sits delicately on the toilet.

SHELBY

I've been spending some time with Gail.

BECKY

What?

121

SHELBY

I took over directing the school play because the director was looking at naked pictures of the girls dancing in the forest.

BECKY

Did they send him back to the priesthood?

SHELBY

No. Well, honestly, I don't know. Anyway, the principal called me to take his place because I was a theater major in college. And Gail said she's living with an older guy named Stan? I just wanted you to know. It didn't seem like a good idea.

BECKY

Well thanks, Shelby, I thought it was a great fucking idea.

SHELBY

So you *knew* she was living with Stan. And you didn't object?

BECKY

If you think I'm going to discuss my parenting choices with you, you're high as a Pilgrim on rye bread.

SHELBY

Funnily enough, I wrote my doctoral thesis discrediting crackpot theories about Salem, like the moldy bread that makes you hallucinate theory.

BECKY

Well, I think biological explanations are usually better than moral ones.

SHELBY

I'm a scholar, my job is to discredit opinions with no evidence, not to explain things.

BECKY

I have a new theory, wanna hear it? It's called the hemorrhoid theory. You know how they examined Rebecca Nurse for witch marks, and found them near her privates? Well, what's a mark of childbirth? Hemorrhoids. And what do you put on hemorrhoids to make 'em go away? *Witch* hazel.

SHELBY

That's actually pretty good. That might be publishable. Maybe we could coauthor a paper. "Protrusions of the female body and medical witchcraft."

BECKY

I think I'll write my own paper. I'll call it "hemorrhoids." I still don't understand why you're here, Shelby.

SHELBY

Well, I thought maybe Gail could come live with me until you get out.

BECKY

What?

SHELBY

She said you might be here for a while—for possession?

BECKY

No, no, I'll be out any day.

SHELBY

Uh-huh. She's a good kid. She's smart. She has potential.

BECKY

I know.

SHELBY

I mean she's really smart. She should go to college, Becky. Have you considered that?

BECKY

Of course I've considered that.

SHELBY

Well, have you *saved up* for that?

BECKY

You fucking fired me!!!

SHELBY

Listen. I don't have kids. I could give Gail some attention. It seems like she could use some attention.

BECKY

Do you really want to take every last thing away from me?

SHELBY

Just trying to help.

BECKY

Well, you're not helping. And the answer is no.

SHELBY

Are you thinking about what would be best for Gail? Or what would be best for Becky?

BECKY

Jesus. You know what, if Gail wants to stay with you until I get out, that's fine. It's up to her. I'll be out any day now.

SHELBY

So I'll ask her.

BECKY

Okay. Make her a grilled cheese sandwich. Do you know how to do that?

SHELBY

I can look it up.

JAILER

Visiting time is over.

Shelby exits.

Scene 8 — Stan Offers a Ritual.

Becky, alone.
She lies on her cot.
Suddenly, Stan appears.
Becky sits up.

BECKY

Stan?

STAN

I just wanted to say, no judgment. Withdrawal sucks.

BECKY

I'm not an addict, Stan.

STAN

Whatever, cold turkey is *rough*. Feel like you're going to die?

BECKY

Yes.

STAN

Like the worst flu you ever had. If flu included walking into hell and the death of your personality?

BECKY

Maybe.

STAN

Mrs. Nurse, I have spoken with my coven about getting you out of jail.

BECKY

You have a coven?

STAN

Yeah. And they want to help.

BECKY

No, I've had enough of witchcraft.

STAN

I knew it!—that charm in my backpack was you.

BECKY

I don't know what you're talking about, Stan.

STAN

Oh, I think you do. That was dark magic, Becky. Ethical witches don't—like—hex people. They help people. I would never just fall out of love with Gail. But you did what you did out of fear. What are you so afraid of?

BECKY

There is a history in our family of young women getting pregnant before they've fully explored their career options.

STAN

Were you pregnant with Gail's mom when you got married?

BECKY

No, she just had a four-month gestation. It was a fucking miracle.

STAN

Right. Well, Gail's not pregnant.

BECKY

See that she's not. Why are you here and not Gail?

STAN

Well, we're both living at Shelby's now—

BECKY

What?!

STAN

And when Gail found out you tried to smuggle in pills, she said, that's it, I'm out, I have no family. She said: You're my family, Stan.

BECKY

Oh, Christ.

STAN

And I don't think it's healthy for Gail to cut herself off entirely from her family like I did. And even though you're mean to me, I like you, Mrs. Nurse.

BECKY

Well, that's very nice, Stan.

STAN

So. I just need a lock of your hair.

BECKY

What?

STAN

For the ritual. To get you out of jail. I have very detailed instructions.

BECKY

Oh, why the hell not?

She gives him a piece of her hair.

STAN

If we're successful with this ritual, I hope you will welcome me into your family with open arms.

BECKY

Into my family?

STAN

I want to ask Gail to marry me.

BECKY

To *marry* you? No, she's sixteen!

STAN

Eventually.

BECKY

No, Stan. You need to get a GED. That's a top fucking priority.

STAN

Sure.

BECKY

Gail needs an IUD, and you need a GED. And there's a lotta other letters you're both gonna need.

STAN

Goodbye, Mrs. Nurse. Good luck. In my experience, the seventh day is the worst.

Stan exits.
Becky, alone.
The stage darkens.

Scene 9 — The Dark Night of the Soul.

Becky alone in the near dark.
She hears voices.

MANY VOICES
(Shelby, the witch, Stan, the magistrate, Gail; whispering, overlapping)
Becky Nurse, we found you, sign our book . . .

BECKY
No, I won't! I won't!

MANY VOICES
Becky Nurse, dance with us . . .

BECKY
Bob! Bob! Help me!

The voice of Bob in the space.

VOICE OF BOB

What is it?

BECKY

Help me Bob their eyes are gleaming!

MANY VOICES

Becky—

VOICE OF BOB

What are you seeing?

BECKY

Devils—witches—

VOICE OF BOB

Tell them to go away.

BECKY

Go away!

VOICE OF BOB

Did they go away?

BECKY

One of them did.

VOICE OF BOB

Tell the others: I love the Lord.

BECKY

I love the Lord.

VOICE OF BOB

Good. Did they go away?

MANY VOICES

Fly away with us, Becky!

BECKY

One just flew away but asked me to fly with her.

VOICE OF BOB

Tell her you only fly with Jesus.

BECKY

I only fly with Jesus!

VOICE OF BOB

Good. Are they gone?

BECKY

Yes, but for a little frog.

VOICE OF BOB

Can you ignore the frog?

BECKY

I think so.

VOICE OF BOB

Good. Now go to sleep.

BECKY

I can't sleep. Bob, where are you?

VOICE OF BOB

I'm in your dream.

Becky dry heaves.

BECKY

I'm throwing up flowers, Bob. I'm throwing up flowers!

VOICE OF BOB

Take a deep breath.

Morning light comes in.

I'm putting butter on your toast.

BECKY

(Feeling warm, radiant) Oh no, oh no—

VOICE OF BOB

What is it!

BECKY

(An epiphany) I'm butter! I can't believe it's not butter is me, no,
I am butter! Gold, melting, loved—

VOICE OF BOB

Becky, put your head against the wall in the jail cell and I'll put
my head against the wall at home and it will be like Pyramus and
Thisbe, but on the toilet.

BECKY

Okay.

*She puts her head against the wall and kisses it. She feels clearer and
clearer.*

VOICE OF BOB

Pretend we're in high school, when we stayed up all night to see
the sunrise.

BECKY

Bob? Remember that night—you climbed up that ladder on the
power plant by the bay, and I said, no, you're going to fall and break
your goddamn neck, but you wanted to see the view? You climbed
up and waved to me. And then you came down, and we swam, at
night, and the power plant was on all night and it glowed. And there
was a tremor in the water. And I was scared, and you kissed me.

Back when Rebecca Nurse was alive it was dark all night long and
you couldn't see what was going on a yard in front of your face.
And they thought they saw witches in the night sky, flying around
on broomsticks. Now it's light all the time but we still can't see a
goddamn thing.

The lights brighten.
Becky, alone.

Scene 10 — Bob Visits Becky.

Morning light.
Becky finally feels clear.
Bob enters.

BECKY

I can't believe you really came.

BOB

Well, I have something to tell you.

BECKY

Me too.

BOB

You first.

BECKY

First, I wanted to say: sorry. I'm sorry I asked you to bring me pills
here. That wasn't right. I put you in danger.

BOB

Well, thank you. I appreciate it. Is that all?

BECKY

No, I felt like I was gonna die last night in here. And you—you
came to me—and— Thank you for visiting my dream and saving
my life.

BOB

You were in my dream last night too.

BECKY

I was?

BOB

Yeah. You asked me if this country was fundamentally fundamen-
talist and then you threw up on me.

BECKY

Is that what you came to tell me?

BOB

No. Listen, Sharon found out about the pills from her second cousin
and she said, why the hell would you even consider doing that?
And I said, I'm a Good Samaritan. And she said, no you're not, you
love her. And I said, yeah, as a friend, as a Christian. And she said,
bullshit Bob, you've loved Becky since you were sixteen years old.
And I said . . . *(Becky listens closely)* I said . . . yeah. Yeah, I have.

So now she wants a divorce.

BECKY

Oh. Um. How do you feel about that?

BOB

I'm here, aren't I?

BECKY

Bob, will you marry me?

BOB

Why should I marry you?

BECKY

Because with all my flaws I love you.
Because we were always meant to be together and our love was
interrupted by a pebble.
Because you are the kindest man I've ever met.

BOB

I'll think about it.

BECKY

Okay.

BOB

(Gently) Why don't you ask me again when you're, you know, out
of jail?

BECKY

Okay, I will.

JAILER

(Over the loudspeaker) Visiting time is over.

BECKY

(To the jailer) Can I hug him?

JAILER

No!

BECKY

Bye, Bob.

BOB

Bye.

Bob exits.

BECKY

(To the jailer) I'll need a piece of paper. And a pencil.

JAILER

What for?

BECKY

I'm going to write out my defense.

Becky writes and writes and writes during the following ritual . . .

Scene 11 — A Ritual in the Dark.

A bell rings.
Stan and Gail perform a ritual.
With a lock of hair.
Let this ritual be specific to your actors.
Music.

                    STAN AND GAIL

Te liberavimus.
Te solvimus.
Te exemimus.
Rebecca et Becky.

Te liberavimus.
Te solvimus.
Te exemimus.
Rebecca et Becky.

                    137

Te liberavimus.
Te solvimus.
Te exemimus.
Rebecca et Becky.

STAN

Instruct the spirits to let Becky and Rebecca free!

GAIL

Let her free!

STAN

And now we dance!

An ecstatic dance.
For some time.
The sounds of ravens cawing and flapping their great wings.
The ritual is complete.
Morning light on Becky.

Scene 12—Court.

The next day.
The jailer becomes a judge.
Becky faces the judge.
Shelby, Stan, Bob and Gail watch.

JUDGE
Becky Nurse. You have one charge of drug possession, and a charge
of breaking and entering, and stealing a—wax works? How do you
plead?

BECKY
Not guilty.

JUDGE
What have you to say in your defense?

BECKY

I sometimes get into trouble for talking too much, judge, but my ancestor, Rebecca Nurse, at the most defining, crucial moment of her life, kept silent, because she couldn't hear the question. She didn't have a lawyer either. So, I made some notes.

JUDGE

Proceed.

She takes a deep breath and looks at her notes.

BECKY

Okay. We're sitting in this courthouse, down the street from the historic Salem courthouse, which is now a Red's Sandwich Shop. Four hundred years ago, the judges used legal language to make simple things seem complicated, and complicated things seem simple.

Funnily enough, one thing I'm not on trial for is witchcraft. Which, Your Honor, I admit, is what I was doing. That's why I was in Shelby's desk.

A gasp from Shelby.

Sorry Shelby. I was trying to get a job. Because I can't seem to get a job to support my family, or get health care, or get food to eat. If I were a fisherwoman I would fish food from the sea, but I don't know how to fish. So I tried to bend the laws of the universe to my will. Which didn't exactly work out for me.

Anyway. Rebecca Nurse had eight children and they accused her of murdering other women's babies; maybe they were jealous, because so many babies died naturally back then. Ann Putnam wanted to talk to her dead child and asked for a spell. You could say all of Salem went crazy because one mother just wanted to speak to her lost child. Back then there was one kind of possession spreading in Salem, and now we have another kind of possession, another epidemic. Another grief that drives you crazy. I should know.

When my daughter Amy had a kidney infection in high school, I gave her one of my pills for the pain. She went from one pill to a pill every day to a pill every hour until eventually, she ground the pills up. She inhaled them. She became them. I locked up the pills and her friends gave her needles. She tried her best to come back from it—in and out of rehab, in and out of jail—I'm sure you've seen her, judge, a skinny little thing, all eyes, in and out of your courtroom—

JUDGE

Yes. I have.

BECKY

As if the courts had anything to do with that kind of pain. I'm betting you've never gone through withdrawal, judge, but I know—now I know—that my daughter was a thousand times braver than me. So.

She was in the Walgreens buying milk with her daughter Gail when she fell over in the aisle. Gail was two, still in diapers, and she tried to wake her mother up. The police called me. And where was I? At the museum giving a goddamn tour. I came. But she was already cold.

I have not been a good model of being a grown-up lately, but I request your clemency, so I can raise my granddaughter.

JUDGE

Are you finished?

BECKY

Almost. The Sacklers should be in fucking jail, I should not be in fucking jail!!

JUDGE

Language.

BECKY

Sorry, judge. I'll be punished for the rest of my life. I don't ask that you pity me—I do ask that you imagine me to be real.

Becky sits down.

JUDGE

Thank you for your sentiments. Unfortunately, the law was not designed to bend to human sentiment. If judges got in the business of listening to stories, we'd 1) never get home for dinner, and 2) we'd never fairly implement the law. Now, you have pled not guilty to breaking and entering, but the video footage shows plainly that—

Shelby, on crutches, stands up.

SHELBY

Excuse me, judge—

JUDGE

What is it?

SHELBY

Judge, the museum would like to drop its charges against Becky Nurse.

Becky is shocked and moved.

BECKY

Shelby—wow.

SHELBY

I realize now—I did not imagine you to be real. I'm sorry.

BECKY

Thank you.

JUDGE

Okay then. Case dismissed.

BECKY

Am I free to go?

JUDGE

Not yet. That was for breaking and entering and stealing a wax Pilgrim. As for as the drug charge—I sentence you to—community service. And rehabilitation.

BECKY

Thank you, judge.

JUDGE

Becky Nurse, you are free to go.

The judge strikes the desk with the gavel.
Bob and Gail approach Becky.
Gail hugs Becky.

Epilogue

Bob, Becky, Stan and Gail on a bench outdoors, near a Walgreens parking lot.
Early spring.
The big sky is revealed.
They each have an ice-cream cone. Preferably a green flavor.
Maybe Gail wears her Crucible *outfit and holds a bouquet of flowers.*
They lick their ice cream for a moment.

BECKY

The play was great. Best Betty I've ever seen, and I've seen a shit ton.

GAIL

Thanks, Grandma.

BECKY

Like I told you, no one is ever lonely when they're in a play. Now, before we go—this Walgreens parking lot is probably where

Rebecca Nurse was hung. And it's where your mom died. So—we
need to do a ritual.

BOB

Thought you were done with witchcraft.

BECKY

A ritual's not witchcraft.

STAN

Witchcraft's what got her out of jail. We did a spell.

BOB

Her own eloquence got her out of jail.

GAIL

How do you know witchcraft didn't produce her eloquence?

BECKY

Do you know what produced my eloquence?

GAIL

What?

BECKY

Love for you, love for Bob—love for—Stan, you're growing on
me. Let's do a ritual. Um . . .

GAIL

Our cones look like witches' hats upside down, we could put them
on the ground, and ritually smash them with our feet.

BOB

Isn't that kind of a waste of ice cream?

GAIL

Nah, smashing the cones will be like smashing all the lies told about
women. It will be really satisfying.

BECKY

Okay. Cones down.

They all put their cones on the ground.

BOB

I heard on PBS that in a Jewish wedding the groom ritually smashes the glass under his foot to scare away evil spirits and remind us that the world is always broken and still we always have to try to make it better. And so let it be with these ice-cream cones.

BECKY

Mazel, Bob.

BOB

Mazel, Becky.

They kiss.

BECKY

Okay. Gail, you want to say a little something?

GAIL

(She takes a big breath) Okay. I used to think there was something really wrong with my mother. And I felt shame. Now I think something is really wrong with the world. And I've always had a mother.

Becky squeezes Gail's hand.
The lights magically get brighter.
For what is the theater but a form of magic,
that comes and goes with the light?

BECKY

Okay. Amy. Bye, sweetheart. Goodbye.
And goodbye, Rebecca Nurse. I'm sorry for what they did to you.

May the accused and the accusers all meet each
other on some open plain in a heaven free of

all this endless bullshit.
And may we love each other
in a world where asking to be loved is the spell
and loving in return is beyond enchantment.

Bob, Becky, Gail and Stan are now a strange, sudden little family.
And the lights get even brighter on this little family.
For what is the theater but a strange, sudden little family?
They hold hands.

And then:
THEY ALL SMASH THEIR CONES.
Blackout.

THE END

AFTERWORD

I had not approached the witchcraft out of nowhere, or from purely social or political considerations. My own marriage of twelve years was teetering and I knew more than I wished to know about where the blame lay. That John Proctor the sinner might overturn his paralyzing personal guilt and become the most forthright voice against the madness around him was a reassurance to me, and, I suppose, an inspiration: it demonstrated that a clear moral outcry could still spring even from an ambiguously unblemished soul. Moving crabwise across the profusion of evidence, I sensed that I had at last found something of myself in it, and a play began to accumulate around this man.

—ARTHUR MILLER, *NEW YORKER*, 1996

PROCTOR
I will make you famous for the whore you are!

ABIGAIL
(Grabs him) Never! I know you, John—you are this moment singing secret hallelujahs that your wife will hang!

PROCTOR
(Throws her down) You mad, murderous bitch!

—ARTHUR MILLER, *THE CRUCIBLE* (screenplay)

In 2022, the last accused witch from Salem was finally pardoned, three hundred and twenty-nine years after her conviction; Massachusetts lawmakers were spurred on by an eighth-grade civics class. In Scotland, a bill is now before parliament to formally pardon the four thousand accused witches (mostly women) who were tortured and killed there. It seems that *Becky Nurse of Salem* is coming at the right time.

✦ ✦ ✦

I started writing this play in 2016 after Trump was elected, and after seeing a production of Arthur Miller's *The Crucible*, when I started to wonder if the depiction of a lustful, deceitful young woman named Abigail stank of fabrication.

Often, a playwright has both a public way into a play and a private way into a play. Ostensibly, Miller's *The Crucible* was about McCarthyism and the blacklist. But privately, it was about Miller's guilt at wanting to sleep with Marilyn Monroe. This bit of truth was passed on to me by the brilliant playwright Branden Jacobs-Jenkins. We were talking about *The Crucible* over a glass of wine at a retreat in Princeton. I was explaining to Branden that I'd recently experienced some rage after seeing a production of *The Crucible*. My rage had nothing to do with its being a masterpiece or not a masterpiece—I think it *is* a masterpiece—but, instead, with my sense that the whole concept of witchery had been redirected toward girls' desires for older married men, which felt like an enormous historical imposition.

"Oh," Branden said. "Didn't you know that Arthur Miller wanted to get with Marilyn Monroe when he wrote that play and he felt guilty about it because he was married and she was young?" I did not. But watching the brilliant documentary Rebecca Miller made about her father, and reading *Timebends*, I saw that, indeed, Miller struggled with his feelings for the younger Marilyn Monroe during the writing of *The Crucible*. Of course, the play was also very much a parable about McCarthyism, about his friend Elia Kazan's betrayal—but the heart of the play is the lust of John Proctor for Abigail Williams. Miller said that he saw a painting of the trials in Salem—of Abigail Williams reaching her hand toward John Proctor—and found a passage about her hand having a burning sensation when it touched Proctor. That was Miller's way in. The real Abigail Williams was eleven years old. In the play, Miller made her seventeen. The real John Proctor was a sixty-year-old tavern keeper. Miller made him an upright farmer, age thirty-five. The real Abigail Williams never turned to prostitution; Miller writes, in *Echoes Down the Corridor*, that legend has it that Abigail grew up to be a whore in Boston. There is no evidence for that line of thinking, nor is there any evidence that she and John Proctor knew each other before the witch trials.

Playwrights deserve the creative liberty to enter their plays with all their emotional heat and history. I do not begrudge anyone a love story, real or fictional. After all, as my friend Ezra (the self-proclaimed maker of the best falafel in the Western world) once told me, every good story must contain a love story. I suppose what strikes me as fundamentally dishonest about *The Crucible* is the mixture of fact and fiction; the copious historical notes, unusually embedded in the stage directions, lead us to believe that we are watching actual history unfold. But we are watching what we always watch onstage—a psychic drama from the mind of a complicated individual relating his psyche to humankind's larger, collective unconscious.

That *The Crucible* is performed at almost every high school—and is, in fact, the way American girls and boys understand the history of Salem—added to my frustration. I thought, all those bonnets, all those Goody this and Goody thats, and, really, Miller just wanted to have sex with Marilyn Monroe! I thought, all those women died, but John Proctor was the hero of the story. I thought, to this day, no one knows why the girls engaged in mass hysteria, but it probably was not the lust of one duplicitous eleven-year-old for a middle-aged barkeep.

For all of these logical reasons, I thought that I would end up writing my own historical drama about the Salem witch trials. But every time I tried to dip my toe into the seventeenth century, my pen came back and told me to stay in my own era. Perhaps because I felt dwarfed by the long shadow cast by Miller's mastery. Or perhaps I wanted to stay in the present moment because I have been undone and fascinated by the language of the witch hunt used by Donald Trump—from his campaign, in which he whipped crowds into a frenzy, yelling, "Lock her up!" with those crowds often replying, "Hang the bitch!" to his term in office, during which he used the expression "witch hunt" hundreds of times, describing himself as the victim. Not since the burning of witches in Europe has the iconography of witchery been used with such base hypocrisy and to such effect.

Although most contemporary historians have dismissed the rye bread explanation for the symptoms of hysteria in Salem as sheer folly, we do know that rye was rare in the New World, and that it was shipped from Europe, often moldering on the long journey. And we also know that Tituba fed rye bread mixed with urine to the girls, trying to get to the bottom of their maladies. It would be ironic if the "cure" for witchcraft was actually a biological deepening and intensifying of the girls' symptoms, which would have subsided on their own after St. Anthony's fire left their bodies. Most contemporary historians eschew a biological explanation, preferring post-traumatic stress from the American Indian Wars, property disputes, and the like as more feasible. I don't know that we'll ever understand why those girls accused their elders of witchcraft. But what we do know is that the accusations were *not* a function of the lust Abigail Williams had for John Proctor.

Speaking of Tituba and the American Indian Wars, I think the historical characters of Tituba and John Indian deserve new plays of their very own. (Two contemporary novels have already been written about Tituba.) Apparently, Tituba may not have come from Barbados, as *The Crucible* suggests, but was, instead, from South America, a member of the Arawak tribe. The magic she was asked to do was not native to Barbados but was European witchcraft already known to the white women who asked her to perform it. The "othering" of Tituba throughout the ages, and the great mystery surrounding her own desires and intentions, deserve investigation. I did not think that story was mine to write.

A note on the opioid crisis. Massachusetts is one of ten states that have the highest casualties for opioid overdoses in the country. In 2017, there were 31.8 deaths per one hundred thousand people in Massachusetts. Approximately sixty-four thousand Americans died of opioid overdoses in 2016, more than died in automobile accidents. It is the largest preventable cause of death for people between the ages of eighteen and thirty-five. This cluster has created what some call a lost generation, flooding the foster care system with their children. The greatest increase in opioid deaths has been attributed to synthetic opioids like fentanyl. In a bizarre karmic loop, or bitter irony, the nineteenth-century opium trade with China, which destroyed the lives of many Chinese citizens, greatly enriched Boston. The money from the trade even helped finance cultural institutions, such as hospitals and libraries in Boston, as well as the Peabody Essex Museum in Salem. Even in nineteenth-century Boston, doctors like Dr. Fitch Edward Oliver warned against the dangers of opium, particularly for women:

> Doomed, often, to a life of disappointment, and, it may be, of physical and mental inaction, and in the smaller and more remote towns . . . deprived of all wholesome social diversion, it is not strange that nervous depression, with all its concomitant evils, should sometimes follow, opium being discreetly selected as the safest and most agreeable remedy.

The current focus on the opioid crisis, which disproportionally affects white Americans, is in stark contrast to the lack of attention, empathy, and resources being directed toward public-health crises that feature fewer white faces on posters.

As for St. Anthony's fire, the disease comes from ergot—a poison produced by a fungus that grows on rye. The condition was named for St. Anthony, who was pursued by hallucinations of the devil in the desert and resisted. Acute and chronic ergotism lead to convulsions, pain in the extremities, and delusions. LSD was originally synthesized from ergot, and medications derived from the fungus are used to treat migraines and Parkinson's disease. I don't wish to add to conspiracy theories by writing this play, nor do I want to ignore a biological explanation for hysteria.

If we are to insist on fact, it should be noted that Gallows Hill does indeed appear to be at the site overlooking a Walgreens in Salem, not a Dunkin' Donuts. Some townspeople and amateur sleuths have claimed that the original site is now a Dunkin' Donuts (a strange fact that led me down the rabbit hole of this play), but the Walgreens was designated in 2016 as the most probable site of the executions. Much of the evidence was wiped away in an attempt to forget, and one of the few historical sites still preserved is the Rebecca Nurse Homestead in Danvers.

I did a reading of this play on July 19, 2019, in Poughkeepsie, and a descendant of Rebecca Nurse, who worked at the theater, wanted to mark the day; in 1692, July 19th was the day that Rebecca Nurse, Sarah Good, and three other women were hanged. Before she died, Nurse said, "Oh, Lord, help me! It is false! I am clear. For my life now lies in your hands." On July 19th, before the reading, we performed a ritual at a very large tree—it is said to have the largest self-supporting branch of any tree in the United States. I cannot tell you what we did around that tree. August 19th is the day that John Proctor was hanged. John Proctor, also an innocent victim, became the cultural symbol of the witch trials (rather than the large group of women who were put to death) as a result of Miller's outsized success in turning Proctor into a tragic hero.

Miller once lived in my neighborhood. Maybe we heard the same fog horns from the water in Brooklyn Heights while thinking about witches. There is a public way into a play and a private way in, like a worm turning over the earth. Earthworms are blind. So, frequently, are writers, especially when they're in the midst of writing. Often, a playwright will never recognize the private way into a play. Sometimes the playwright knows and keeps it secret. Sometimes the playwright does not know while writing but realizes, with some embarrassment, at the first preview, and blushes. Sometimes the playwright does not know while writing but realizes ten years later, and, like the great Arthur Miller, writes about it in a very thick memoir. Let playwrights have their secrets, their private lusts, their compulsions—but do let us free Abigail Williams from her manufactured lust for John Proctor. When John Proctor says, "It is a whore!" and the "it" is a child called Abigail, let us consider that the real historical child was neither an "it" nor a whore.

As for my own private reason for writing this particular play, I either don't know or I will never tell.

—*Sarah Ruhl*
Provincetown, MA

ACKNOWLEDGMENTS

Huge thanks to Rebecca Taichman for our long-term artistic collaboration and for helming the New York production so beautifully. Hedgebrook and the McCarter Theatre and Berkeley Repertory Theatre, Ground Floor, Nashville Repertory Theatre, for time, space, and radical hospitality. Amy Wheeler. Emily Mann. Tony Taccone. Frances McDormand. Kathryn Schultz. Honor Moore. Polly Noonan. The Pickle Council—Kathleen Tolan, Andy Bragen, Jorge Cortiñas. Madeleine Oldham. Sarah Rose Leonard. René Copeland. Anne Kauffman. Sarah Benson. Nicholas Dawidoff. Robin DeRosa. Paula Vogel. Anne Cattaneo. André Bishop. Lincoln Center Theater. NYSF and Johanna Pfaelzer. Lisa Benner. Jody Rich. Len Berkman. Mandy Greenfield and Williamstown. P. Carl. Anne Harrigan. Jessica Hecht. The first glorious cast at Berkeley Repertory Theatre: Pamela, Owen, Naian, Adrian, Elissa, Ruibo, Rod. Pamela Reed, I am forever indebted to you for your indelible incarnation. The glorious cast at Lincoln Center Theater: Didi, Alicia, Bernie, Julian, Candy, Tina, and Tom. Didi—you are a goddess. And always, Tony Charuvastra.

Books and resources that have been hugely helpful: Robin DeRosa's *The Making of Salem: The Witch Trials in History, Fiction and Tourism*; Margo Burns's resources on *The Crucible* and Salem; all the work on Salem of Marilynne K. Roach; *The Witches* by Stacy Schiff; *In Pain: A Bioethicist's Personal Struggle with Opioids* by Travis Rieder; *Hallucinations* by Oliver Sacks.

◆ ◆ ◆

Suzzy Roche composed this beautiful song for the New York production, and we used it during Stan and Gail's ritual.

"Song for Becky" by Suzzy Roche

When the petals fall from the bloom
And you're chasing your demons to the moon

Mixing up potions as thick as your blood
Honey, I'm just around the bend
OOH I'm just around the bend

Grief makes you crazy
Well, I oughta know
There are scars on my soul
I could show you

You've got to fly with the raven
You've got to hear as she sings

There's a ghost in your heart
Pinning your wings
Honey, give 'em the magic wand
OOH give 'em the magic wand

When the petals fall from the bloom
And you're running from CVS to the moon

Dunking your donuts in all the wrong cups
Honey, you'll go around the bend

OOOH, oh my darling what then

Lyrics reprinted by courtesy of Suzzy Roche.